THE SURRENDERED CHRISTIAN ATHLETE

BY
BRANT TOLSMA

The Surrendered Christian Athlete

by

Brant Tolsma

© 2001

Library of Congress Control Number: 2001094787

ISBN: 1-890306-34-7

Warwick **H**ouse

Publishing
720 Court Street
Lynchburg, VA 24504

Dedication

Since I do not anticipate writing another book, I would like to make several dedications of this work: First of all, to my father Jacob, who from my earliest childhood taught me about Jesus and modeled Him to me; to my wonderful wife Nancy and our six children, who always accept and love me through success and failure; to my assistant coaches, who share my heart, and the many athletes who have helped teach me these lessons; and most of all, to Jesus Christ, the perfect model for the surrendered Christian athlete.

TABLE OF CONTENTS

Foreword

The Eye of the Heart

What would happen to a gifted athlete if he trained his heart with the same dedication as he trained his body? As we watched Michael Jordan, Tiger Woods, Mike Singletary, Lance Armstrong, Reggie White and a precious handful of the truly stellar athletes write new parameters in the book of success, we were captured by that look in their eyes...that singular, microscopic focus that somehow we knew came straight from their heart.

The great coaches across America ask, "How can we instill that kind of eye of the heart into our athletes? If we could, going undefeated would be attainable."

This book and its author do just that. Brant Tolsma is an author who trains the heart because he is one of those who not only has that kind of heart, but he is able to convince athletes to train their hearts in a similar manner.

"Christ in you, the hope of glory" is his theme. "Run to win" is his motivation. "Play for Him," is his audience.

Any athlete, any team, any coach will be much better for studying this invaluable book. An "eye of the heart" with a much clearer vision will undoubtedly be the result.

Dr. Joe White, President
Kanakuk Kamps

To become a successful athlete or coach it is imperative to recognize the complicated dynamics involved in motivation for performance. This is the best resource I have ever read for providing the simplistic truth of biblical principles needed to open the door for maximum training and performance. Our team study and application of these principles brought a clear refreshing direction toward motivation and God's blessings. Needless to say, our team's performance reached a higher level. God's Word never returns void.

Carey Green
Head Women's Basketball Coach
Liberty University

Coach Tolsma has brilliantly captured the achievements, complacencies and disappointments of the many coaches and athletes he has encountered over the years. Coach's ability to express these experiences in writing will serve as a biblical blueprint for Christian athletes to follow when faced with the highs and lows of their journey. This book is a must read for any person struggling with the I, me, my, mine syndrome. I am extremely proud of this man of God.

James E. McKnight
Wide Receiver
Miami Dolphins

In *The Surrendered Christian Athlete*, Dr. Brant Tolsma reveals God's secret to success: if one trains with all his heart, all his mind, and all his soul, focuses on the greatness of Christ and believes that God can achieve extraordinary results with ordinary people, magnificent feats will be accomplished.

Practical chapters range from motivational techniques to piquing one's attitude through personal anecdotes while stimulating the coach and athlete to raise their competitive bar of excellence as they receive God's exponential rewards for obedience. It is a belief system for the tough-minded Christian who is willing to surrender to a tenderhearted Christ for His benefits.

The Surrendered Christian Athlete is a must read for those who are excited about acquiring spiritual power for achieving goals beyond themselves. I highly recommend the text.

Mel Hankinson
Head Men's Basketball Coach
Liberty University

Chapter 1
The Sovereignty of God

The top thirteen decathlon competitors were led into the glare of the lights at the Los Angeles Coliseum. This was to be the last event of a very busy day of competition at the 1984 Olympic track and field trials. The sun had set several hours earlier and most of the crowd had already left the arena. Less than one thousand true decathlon fans and sportswriters remained in the 92,000-seat stadium, eager to witness this final event. Two heats of the 1500m run, the tenth and final event of the decathlon, had just been completed for the rest of the thirty-nine athletes who had survived the two-day ordeal. Fourteen of the overly large starting field of fifty-three had already dropped out, having experienced the reality of their shattered dreams. The results of this final race would set the 1984 U.S. Olympic decathlon team.

As this group of America's "greatest athletes" strode onto the track, the fatigue of the long two-day competition seemed to evaporate into the electricity that filled the arena. Twelve of the athletes jogged, stretched, and sprinted, trying to complete the final part of the warm-up which had been limited by the confines of the athlete holding room. Only one athlete showed no sign of final preparation as he walked slowly onto the track. He was an amazingly chiseled specimen of a decathlete, the kind that one would expect to win the title of "the world's greatest athlete." In his early twenties, he stood 6'1" at 195 pounds with only 3 percent body fat. His huge chest, broad shoulders and narrow waist made it no surprise that he could bench-press 400 pounds. He had also long jumped over 25', high jumped over 7', and put the shot over 50'. However, the conservation in his movements and the large wrap on his left thigh were indications that something was not right.

As he walked slowly toward the starting line, fear gripped his young coach who sat alone in a circle of empty seats. His mind was racing. *What is he doing? Why isn't he preparing for the race? What is wrong with his leg? What is he going to do in this race?* Because of the large crowd of spectators that had filled the stands most of the day and the structured nature of the meet, the coach and athlete had not been able to have any contact since the day began. A blast from the starting pistol broke the coach's thoughts and suddenly most of his questions were answered. A dozen athletes burst from the starting line into relaxed but fast gaits, while this injured athlete was immediately left behind as he labored into a slow, limping jog.

The coach's mind quickly became active again. What is O.V. doing? Why is he running so slow, and if that is the best he can do, why is he running at all? He will receive no points for a run at this pace. His coach had given Orville the nickname "O.V." and it had stuck. All his track friends called him O.V. Orville and his coach had spent countless hours together in the past three years preparing for this day. Though one of the youngest athletes in the field, O.V. came to the meet with the third highest score in the country and he was improving rapidly, so he and his coach both believed that he would make the Olympic team. He had been called America's best decathlon hope for the future by the U.S. decathlon coordinator. However, this meet had not gone according to plan. In the first event, the 100m dash, O.V.'s heat experienced the strongest head wind of all seven heats. Running into a two-meter per second wind, he ran 11.37 rather than his usual sub 11. His long jump was also short of the 24'+ marks that had become commonplace. A solid shot put and high jump preceded a fair 400-meter dash that left him in eighth place at the end of the first day.

Determined to use the second day to move back into contention for the Olympic team, Orville attacked the hurdles, one of his best events, with a reckless abandonment. He moved well over several hurdles when, suddenly, a hamstring muscle, which had side-lined him only three months earlier, again failed the test. Nevertheless, he managed to finish the race with a respectable, though certainly not exciting time. A reasonable discus throw was possible with the injury, but the pole vault presented problems. O.V. did manage one clearance at his opening height of 12'5", but he then passed to 14'1". His coach saw his obvious difficulty on the runway, but he did not know what was taking place. Failure at that height dropped Orville several places in the standings. When he showed up for the javelin with his thigh in a bandage, his coach received his first clue of the problem. A strong javelin throw well beyond 200' raised his standing so that he was thirteenth going into the final event. The top thirteen were grouped to run the final heat, which was now being nationally televised.

With the cameras rolling, O.V. was falling further and further behind. He was limping along at half the speed of the field and as he passed one lap, the leaders were already closing in to lap him. Orville moved into lane two, deferring lane one out of courtesy to those really in the race, and his coach began to try to think of ways to get him off the track to put an end to this humiliation. He considered jumping over the rail and running out on the track to pull him off, but he was too embarrassed to do that. He yelled for him to hang it up, but, as if in a daze, O.V. plodded on. Perhaps people would continue to ignore Orville, as they appeared to be making great efforts to do. The coach looked for a place to hide, but there was none. This was certainly the most embarrassing experience of the young coach's life.

This coach had been on a mission for several years. He had been only a fair athlete himself despite his hyper-activity, but his love for athletics, challenges and variety caused the decathlon to have great appeal to him. Lacking opportunity, he had never done a decathlon himself until he was twenty-seven years old, but even then he prayed to God for the talent to excel, offering God the promise that he would give Him the glory. The usual rigors of excelling in engineering school had been no problem for him, but the difficulty he encountered excelling in track and field made it even more exciting and challenging to him. His love of athletics and his scientifically oriented mind had lured him to study the biomechanics of sports, and when he received his Ph.D. in that field at age twenty-nine, he was still an unfulfilled athlete. His degrees had produced the offers to teach in college, but it was the opportunity to coach a track team at an NCAA Division I school that led him to sign a contract at a college that was relatively unknown in track circles. Campbell University had never had a national qualifier, much less an All-American. The four-lane asphalt track at the school had not deterred this young coach's enthusiasm and he approached his job with an undaunted passion. He was determined to put that small school on the track map, and Orville proved to be the one to do it. Within three years O.V. had risen from a novice to become NCAA Division I decathlon runner-up, and now, a year later, he was one of the best in the country. However, at the present time he was enduring a lesson in humiliation and his coach could not understand why. As one by one the entire field left him for a second time, O.V. moved back into lane one and plodded on. Spectators continued to ignore him like a handicapped person is sometimes awkwardly ignored on an elevator. Only one person seemed to be paying him any attention, and that was another decathlete named Fred Dixon, who had completed his performance in an earlier heat.

Fred's thinning hair gave away the fact that he was not a young athlete. Fred was a veteran and a two-time Olympian trying to make his third Olympic team. At thirty-four years of age and with a wife and children, he had years before given up decathlon training. However, as an Olympic Games in his own backyard drew nearer, this Christian Californian found himself asking God if it would be all right if he gave it one more try. He began a relatively brief but intense training program, which prepared him to produce one of the highest scores in the country shortly before the Olympic Trials.

To the surprise of many, Fred Dixon had performed very well on day one and had retired to his own home at the end of the first day with the overall lead. He had continued well through the hurdles, an event that had spelled disaster for him at the 1976 Olympics when he had been a major medal contender with Bruce Jenner.

This time, however, tragedy struck in the discus ring. Despite throwing very far, all three of his attempts were ruled foul for different reasons. He received no points for that event and all hopes of making the team were destroyed. Fred tried to regroup for the pole vault, but the psychological beating he had taken in the discus carried over to the pole vault and he missed his opening height three times, receiving zero points in that event as well. After so much sudden bad fortune, Fred retired to the athlete resting area to try to organize his thoughts and emotions. He lay down beside Orville, who was there icing his injured hamstring.

Orville's coach knew about all the better competitors in the meet and he had earlier told O.V. that Fred Dixon was a Christian. Fred had long been open and outspoken about his faith. Feeling very discouraged, Orville introduced himself and said, "I understand that you're a Christian. So am I." Orville wanted to talk, but Fred didn't. Orville tried to explain his shattered dreams and told Fred that he was dropping out of the decathlon after the javelin. Fred later recounted that Orville came to him seeking godly counsel from a more mature Christian brother, but Fred, understandably wrapped up in his own woes, failed to give Spirit-led counsel. Instead, Fred said, "Yeah, Orville, we're both disappointed. There is no point in going on. I'm out of here," and he got up and went to the head official to withdraw from the meet. After finding his wife and his car, he traveled many miles on the freeway toward home.

Away from the coliseum and the stress of the meet, Fred began to hear the still, small voice that is known to those who walk with the Lord. *You just counseled that young Christian guy and told him that it is okay to quit.* He tried to push the thought out of his mind, but it came back. *Your Christian brother came to you seeking approval of a wrong decision, and you confirmed him in that wrong decision.* As he continued down the highway, Fred silently argued with that voice. *I can't go back now. It's too late. What will I tell my wife? Look at her. I've put her through an emotional ringer already. Besides, the javelin will be over by now. It's too late.* Another exit passed, and then the Spirit of God won. Mustering up his courage, he turned to his wife and said, "I have to go back." Despite her shock and the added turmoil that this would add to her day, a few minutes later they were speeding back toward the L.A. Coliseum. Once back at the stadium, Fred quickly found the official who had allowed him to withdraw and with some fast-talking and his reputation as the "dean of American decathletes," he got back in the meet just in time for the final javelin throws. It was then that he truly recognized that this occurrence was certainly of the Lord. With his javelin throw done, he went on a search for Orville.

Fred found Orville resting in the tent, again icing his swollen hamstring. Orville was by then rather comfortable with the fact that he would not be running the 1500m. Orville hated that event anyway as it was definitely his worst event and it was the most painful as well. He had run his personal record of 4:39 just a few weeks earlier, but a performance like that was certainly now impossible. Even such a performance would not bring him into contention to make the Olympic team. There was nothing to be gained by running it at this point. As he relaxed in the tent, "enjoying" the peace that comes when something is over even if it hasn't turned out the way it was planned, Fred ran up to him. "Orville, I was wrong. You've got to run the 1500m. You can do it. Even if you have to crawl, you've got to finish this decathlon. I'll be proud of you; your kids will be proud of you someday." Orville put up a good argument. "I've tried to run and I can't. My hamstring is all swollen. I've been icing it and it's real stiff." However, the Spirit of God had by then convinced Fred that this was the right thing to do and he was determined that Orville would run the 1500m.

When Fred left to run his own 1500m, the first heat, Orville knew that he had to finish this decathlon. To finish a decathlon, however, one must only start the 1500m, not finish it. Orville began to talk with officials about getting into the second heat instead of the final heat, thinking that he could start and then walk off the track with very little notice. However, the officials would not cooperate with Orville. After a strong effort in which the famous decathlon announcer Frank Zarnowski acknowledged Fred's many decathlon accomplishments spanning almost two decades, a winded but happy Fred returned to Orville, now as a representative of the Almighty God Himself. "Orville, you are going to run the 1500m." Obedience to the voice of God is something that a Christian does well to learn. Though at first reluctant, Fred had obeyed. Now, even more reluctantly, Orville was obeying.

Being lapped in a 1500m is certainly a rare happening, but now a very long three-hundred meters later, the leaders were again closing in on Orville. His coach began to wonder if they would pass him again, but they would not because they were approaching the finish line. Several were sprinting with all their energy competing for those coveted Olympic team berths. By the time the last healthy runner finished, Orville was still over one hundred meters from the finish line. With only a few exceptions, spectators were still ignoring him. However, as he drew near to the finish line, the fans began to clap for him, as they often do for the last finisher, giving him the token polite applause. When he reached the finish line, nearly everyone felt that a long, hard day was now over.

It was then that one of the most awkward moments in sports took place. Orville continued "running." He still had a lap to go. The fans had turned their token attention to Orville, but how could they watch this slow, agonizing jog for three more minutes? As he continued into the last lap, seconds seemed like minutes in the stadium. Orville's coach sat with his head between his hands. He didn't know what to do, and neither did the rest of the remaining spectators.

After many long, uncomfortable seconds, the strong voice of Frank Zarnowski broke the painful silence. "Ladies and gentlemen, on the track we have an athlete, obviously injured, who desires to fulfill his commitment to the decathlon." Those twenty-one words totally changed the mood in the Los Angeles Coliseum. Where people had been trying to ignore this athlete, they now suddenly began to empathize with him. Where they had just seen a pitiful, handicapped young man, they now saw a noble warrior striving with his last ounce of courage to fulfill a worthy cause. Where they had seen a victim, they now saw a hero. All who had remained for this event were drawn into the emotion of the moment. As each spectator felt his heart being pulled into Orville's ordeal, the familiar sound of the *Chariots of Fire* theme burst out over the stadium's public address system. The beat of the music seemed to match the shuffle of Orville's legs and people began to cheer and clap for him. Tears welled up in the eyes of many spectators and they knew they were observing a great moment in sport. As he rounded the final curve, with the *Chariots of Fire* theme still playing in the background, Frank Zarnowski's strong, yet emotional, voice again pierced the air. "Ask not for victory. Ask only for courage. For if you endure the struggle, you bring honor to yourself. But more importantly, you bring honor to us all." As Orville approached the finish line, Frank said, "Ladies and gentlemen, this is Orville Peterson. Remember that name in 1988." The national television coverage showed him finishing and called him the "epitome of a decathlete."

When he crossed the finish line, O.V. was immediately swarmed by the press. Three athletes had just made the USA Olympic team, but Orville Peterson was the story of interest at that moment. Everyone wanted to know who he was and what motivated him to continue on when there was no apparent reward. Orville's 1500-meter time of 9:44.80 was worth zero points and he dropped to thirty-second place, but his performance was the story that went out to the newspapers across the country. Orville received many times more press coverage than there had ever been for any of his previous fine decathlons. After recounting the story, Gordon Morris of the *Los Angeles Times* wrote: "Yet for ten stirring minutes Orville Peterson was a champion—providing shining testimony that, through determined men and women like him, America's long tradition of athletic excellence will never be in jeopardy." Jack Wilkinson of the *Atlanta Constitution* wrote of Orville: "He finished. He needed to run the 1500m in 6:39.6 to score a single point. He got nothing. He ran 9:44.80. But he got everything. He reminded us that the true Olympic spirit isn't hot pink Spandex body suits, under the table payments and the official sparkling water of the Olympics. And he brought honor to us all." The story touched countless people. One person wrote to the *L.A. Times* suggesting that Orville should be asked to carry the flag in the Olympic Games opening ceremony.

Orville did later win the U.S. Olympic Festival and the National Pentathlon Championship, but that moment on a still June evening in Los Angeles was his greatest moment. God took Orville Peterson's lowest moment, his time of greatest weakness, and turned it into his greatest moment. It was not the tremendous "don't quit" attitude of Orville. He dropped out of many decathlons before and after that one, and he wanted to drop out of that one too. It was not his young coach, now a middle-aged coach who is the author of this book. He would have prevented that moment if he could. It was not even Fred Dixon, who came ever so close to quitting himself. It was God. God has a plan and He will accomplish His plan. His plan involves the lives of men and women, boys and girls. He loves the crown of His creation, mankind, and He wants to work in and through them. "For the eyes of the Lord search back and forth across the whole earth, looking for people whose hearts are perfect toward Him, so that He can show His great power in helping them." (II Chr. 16:9 TLB) You can be assured that "…what has been determined must take place." (Dan. 11:36b NIV)

God has a plan for your life. His plan is far better than your own plan. He wants to unleash His "great power" to help you fulfill

His plan. You have been uniquely created so that you are capable of completing the plan He has for you. You have received, are receiving, or will receive all the opportunities that you need to fulfill His plan for your life, as long as you do not fight against His will. But, you must work at "perfecting your heart toward Him."

God has the ability and interest in working out every detail in your life. His ability comes from His power. "O Lord God…Yours is the mighty power and glory and victory and majesty. Everything in the heavens and earth is yours, O Lord, and this is your kingdom. We adore you as being in control of everything. Riches and honor come from you alone, and you are the Ruler of all mankind; your hand controls power and might, and it is at your discretion that men are made great and given strength." (I Chr. 29:11-12 TLB) His interest comes from His love. "But God…loved us so much that even though we were spiritually dead and doomed by our sins, he gave us back our lives again when he raised Christ from the dead…and lifted us up from the grave into glory along with Christ." (Eph. 2:4-6)

God's power and His love are both great beyond our comprehension. They reach into every detail of your life. "Do not two sparrows sell for a penny? And not one of them falls to the ground apart from the will of your Father. As for you, the hairs of your head are all numbered. Have no fear, then; you are of more consequence than many sparrows." (Matt. 10:29-31 ML) God controls the wind and the sea. "…even the wind and the sea obey Him." (Matt. 8:27 ML) He controls the sun and the rain "…for He makes the sun to rise on the evil and the good and He pours rain upon the just and the unjust." (Matt. 5:45 ML) The God of this entire universe, the creator of every giant star and every tiny atom, is fully capable of working out His will in your life down to the minutest detail. "I know that Thou canst do all things, and that no plans of Thine can be foiled." (Job 42:2 ML) "…with God all things are possible."

(Matt. 19:26) He has said, "I am the LORD, the God of all mankind. Is anything too hard for me?" (Jer. 32:27 NIV)

Yet, despite His ability to control everything including you, God still gave you your own free will. You can choose to allow the Almighty, sovereign God to direct your life, or you can choose to go your own way. If God did not give you your own free will, how could you ever choose to love Him? Your love for Him only has meaning when it is your choice. If you love Him, you will desire to follow Him and obey Him. Your heart will be pure. God will test you to see what is in your heart. "But O my God, I know that Thou dost test the heart and dost take pleasure in what is right...." (I Chr. 29:17 ML) Is your heart perfect toward God, or are you under the control of the world, the flesh, and the devil?

The surrendered Christian athlete has surrendered his will to Christ. He knows that God is Almighty and Sovereign. He knows that God's will for his life is better than his own will and he desires with his whole heart for God to have His will in his life. He knows that he is an athlete because God has blessed him with athletic ability and opportunities to develop those talents. He knows that God gave him these abilities and opportunities for a purpose and that God wants him to use these gifts to fulfill God's plan in his life. He knows that God can use him in victory or in defeat. He is ready to be used by God in whatever way God chooses and he rejoices in the knowledge that God will use him. He gladly surrenders his will to his Almighty, Sovereign God. Don't you want to be a surrendered Christian athlete?

Chapter 2
The Lordship of Christ

His difficult race was now nearly over. It took all his strength to climb the steep road leading to the finish. He could barely make it in his weakened state. The previous several hours had been an agonizing ordeal that had left him drained, but now his goal lay just a short distance ahead. The ultimate purpose of his life was soon to be accomplished. So, he pressed on with the determined will of the world's greatest athlete. He would endure to the end. Achieving the prize would cost him his life.

He was the greatest athlete that ever lived. Though not an athlete in the traditional sense of the word, he certainly fit the definition of one who contests for a prize. He was at the center of the most important contest in history, the contest between the forces of good and the forces of evil. He was contesting for the souls of men. By enduring the struggle, he would bring honor to himself and life to us all. The latter goal was his motivation. Many athletes have put aside their own immediate desires and endured hardship and suffering for the greater good, for the final prize. Jesus Christ, however, experienced this at a level that no other athlete has ever known. "...being in very nature God...(He) made Himself nothing, taking the very nature of a servant, being made in human likeness.... He humbled himself and became obedient to death—even death on a cross. Therefore, God exalted Him to the highest place and gave Him the name that is above every name, that at the name of Jesus every knee should bow, in heaven and on earth and under the earth, and every tongue confess that Jesus Christ is Lord to the glory of God the Father." (Phil. 2:6-11 NIV) "...all who go down to the dust will kneel before Him." (Psalm 22:29b NIV)

The day is coming when those who have not known Jesus as Lord in this life will call Him Lord, for they will say, "Lord, when did we see you hungry or thirsty or a stranger or needing clothes or sick or in prison, and did not help you?" (Matt. 25:44) How blessed are those who recognize His Lordship now.

Whether or not you recognize it, Jesus Christ is indeed Lord. He is Lord of creation, for "all things were created by Him and for Him." (Col. 1:16 NIV) He is Lord in heaven, for the angels proclaim, "Worthy is the Lamb who was slain, to receive power and wealth and wisdom and strength and honor and glory and praise." (Rev. 5:12 NIV) Even the demons recognize Him as Lord. Luke 4 tells the story of a demon possessed man who, seeing Jesus, cried out, "Ha! What do you want with us, Jesus of Nazareth? Have you come to destroy us? I know who you are—the Holy One of God!" (Luke 4: 34 NIV) Yet many on earth do not recognize Him, for Satan has "blinded their eyes and deadened their hearts, so that they can neither see with their eyes, nor understand with their hearts…." (John 12: 40 NIV) Or again in the words of Paul, "The god of this age has blinded the minds of unbelievers, so that they cannot see the light of the gospel of the glory of Christ, who is the image of God." (II Cor. 4: 18 NIV)

This was not only true in Bible times, but it is also true today. Satan is still working hard trying to sell his lies. We hear them in the advertising that lures us to buy products. *You, you're the one. Do your own thing. Grab all the gusto. You deserve a break today.* The world tells you that you belong on the throne of your life. There is no place for surrendering your own will. You should be the lord of your own life. You should be able to sing with Frank Sinatra, "I did it my way."

Yet, there are many things that we gladly surrender to God. If God gave you the job of keeping all the planets and their moons moving on the correct paths, you would probably try to return the job to Him saying, "You created all these things. You know better than I do how to control them. You take care of it." Then, why are we so reluctant to do this with our own lives? We want to control them ourselves. We want to fulfill our own little agenda and we somehow think that if we can do that, we will be happy.

To our surprise, real joy comes only when we turn the reins of our lives over to Jesus Christ. If we knew Christ in all His "power and wealth and wisdom and strength and honor and glory" we would not hesitate to place Him on the throne of our lives. We would gladly make Jesus Lord of our lives, and when we did we would experience a freedom, a peace, and a joy that cannot be matched by the world.

However, surrendering is against our human nature and it is not easy for us. Surrendering to the Lordship of Christ is not a one-time, quick, easy decision. Recognizing Jesus as Lord and learning to turn control of our lives over to Him is a lifetime process. There are areas of our lives that we are eager to submit to His Lordship, but then there are usually other areas that we are very reluctant to turn over to Him.

In the well-known tract, *My Heart, Christ's Home*, Dr. Robert Munger tells what happened after he invited Jesus Christ into his heart. "In the joy of this new-found relationship I said to Jesus Christ, 'Lord, I want this heart of mine to be Yours. I want to have You settle down here and be perfectly at home. Everything I have belongs to You. Let me show You around.'" As he brought Jesus into the various rooms of his house, he found that there were things that he had to change if Jesus was going to live there. After making many changes in each room of the house, he finally gave Jesus comfortable access to the entire house, except for one small closet. The story concludes,

One day I found Him waiting for me at the door. There was an arresting look in His eye, and He said to me as I entered, "There is a peculiar odor in the house. Something is dead around here. It's upstairs. I'm sure it is in the hall closet." As soon as He said the words, I knew what He was talking about. Yes, there was a small hall closet up there on the landing, just a few feet square. In that closet, behind lock and key, I had one or two little personal things that I did not want Christ to see. I knew they were dead and rotting things, and I wanted them so for myself that I was afraid to admit they were there.

I went up with Him. As we mounted the stairs, the odor became stronger and stronger. He pointed to the door. I was angry. That's the only way I can put it. I had given Him access to the library, the dining room, the drawing room, the workshop, the rumpus room, and now He was asking me about a little two-by-four closet. I said inwardly, this is too much. I am not going to give Him the key.

Said He, reading my thoughts, "If you think I'm going to stay up here on the second floor with this odor, you are mistaken. I will go out on the porch."

I saw Him start down the stairs. My resistance collapsed. When one comes to know and love Christ, the worst thing that can happen is to sense His companionship withdrawing. I had to surrender.

"I'll give you the key," I said sadly, "but You will have to open up the closet and clean it out. I haven't the strength to do it." "Just give Me the key," He said. "Authorize Me to take care of that closet and I will."

With trembling fingers I passed the key to Him. He took it, walked over to the door, opened it, entered, took out all the putrefying stuff that was rotting there, and threw it away. Then He cleaned the closet and painted it. It was done in a moment's time. Oh, what victory and release to have that dead thing out of my life!

A thought came to me. Lord, is there any chance that You would take over the management of the whole house and operate it for me as You did that closet? Would You take the responsibility to keep my life what it ought to be?

His face lightened up as He replied, "Certainly, that is what I want to do. You cannot be a victorious Christian in your own strength. Let Me do it through you and for you. That is the way. But," He added slowly, "I am just a guest. I have no authority to proceed, since the property is not mine." Dropping to my knees, I said, "Lord. You have been a guest and I have been the host. From now on I am going to be the servant. You are going to be the Lord."

Running as fast as I could to the strongbox, I took out the title deed to the house describing its properties, assets and liabilities. I eagerly signed the house over to Him alone for time and eternity. "Here," I said. "Here it is, all that I am and have, forever. Now You run the house. I'll just remain with You as a servant and friend."

Things are different since Jesus Christ has settled down and has made His home in my heart.

Things will be different in the life of any athlete who surrenders his will, his athletics and his life to the Lordship of Christ. His athletics will change. His life will change. Both will become immeasurably better. This can be true for you. You can become the surrendered Christian athlete. If you do, you will become what God created you to be. Put Jesus on the throne of your life and victory will be guaranteed. Make Him the Lord of your life and your life will have an impact for eternity. Begin the work of becoming a surrendered Christian athlete today.

Chapter 3
The Principle of Talents

The back of the T-shirt read, "Second place is first loser." It expressed the sentiment of so many athletes. "Winning is what athletics is all about. Second place isn't good enough. I have to be the best." Certainly it is true that most successful athletes have a strong desire to be the best. Perhaps one reason that you are reading this book is because you have that desire, and that is not necessarily wrong. If you work very hard and become the best at a certain level, you will be challenged to move up to a new, higher level of competition and there you will begin the struggle again, trying to become the best at this more difficult level. If you excel at the conference level, you will qualify for the district championship. Faring well there will advance you to regionals. Many are eliminated there but the best go on to the state. Then there are often other levels beyond state. And so it goes. The level you can reach, that is, how good an athlete you will ever become, depends upon only two things: (1) how much innate ability you have or, in other words, how great are your God-given talents, and (2) how much you are able to develop and multiply those talents.

Jesus told the parable of the talents in Matthew 25. While talking about the kingdom of God, Jesus said, "It will be like a man going on a journey, who called his servants and entrusted his property to them. To one he gave five talents, to another two talents, and to another one talent, each according to his ability." (Matt. 25:14-15)

The man in authority, that is, the master, had some knowledge about his servants' abilities even before his trip, and based upon his impression of these abilities, he entrusted varying amounts of his property to them. The man who was given five talents and the man given two talents both went to work "at once," working to multiply those talents. They began immediately to show that the master's trust in them was justified. However, the man given only one talent went and dug a hole in the ground and hid his master's money. He did not waste it. He actually did some work—dug a hole to keep it safe—so that he would have it to return when his master came back. He was not like the prodigal son of Luke 15 who wasted his inheritance in riotous living. In fact, the Scriptures do not record that the master even told the servants to multiply what he entrusted to them. However, the servants knew that their master would expect his money back when he returned and that he would also demand something more in return. However, the servant who was given only one talent was afraid of failure, afraid that he might lose his master's money. He did not want to take the risk and he did not want to do the work.

After a long time the master returned and demanded an accounting from his servants. The first servant met him with ten talents and the second with four talents, both having doubled the master's investment. To each of those servants the master spoke exactly the same words. "Well done, good and faithful servant! You have been faithful with a few things; I will put you in charge of many things. Come and share your master's happiness!" (Matt. 25:21,23) There was no difference in the master's response to the servant given five talents or the one given two talents. Both servants had done well, earning 100 percent profit, and they were commended for being faithful. Both had increased their master's trust in them and both were given a promise of increased opportunity in the future. Both were invited to share in their master's happiness.

The master refers to both the five talents and the two talents as "a few things." The exact number of talents is not the issue. The servants' faithfulness is the issue. More talents simply means more responsibility, for "much is required from those to whom much is given, for their responsibility is greater." (Luke 12:48 TLB) Yet, so often people in athletics glorify someone for the amount of talent he has been given. They honor the athlete for the gifts he has received, sometimes worshiping "created things rather than the Creator." (Romans 1:25 NIV)

God's interest, however, is in what is done with what has been given and, even more importantly, what is the attitude of the heart of the athlete seeking to multiply his talents. Is he working hard for the joy of returning multiplied talents to the Master? Does he desire the opportunity to serve the Master in a greater way? Does he want to bring his Master happiness and to share in that happiness? This is the servant that the master commends and calls "good and faithful."

On the contrary, the third servant is called "wicked and lazy." By his own admission, he knew that the master was demanding and would be expecting more than his own one talent when he returned. Yet, despite this knowledge, he was not faithful to his master. He not only failed to fulfill his master's wishes, he even failed to try to satisfy them. Therefore, that servant lost what he was given, lost his opportunity for further service, and was cast out from the master's presence.

This parable of the Lord places several questions before you as a Christian athlete. First, what are the talents that God has given to you? Surely, they are many, perhaps so many that you cannot wholeheartedly pursue multiplying all of them. As an athlete, you may have some ability and experience in dozens of sports, but you cannot and should not attempt to reach your maximum potential in all of them. Rather, as God reveals His will to you, you should gradually narrow down your areas of concentration so that you can most effectively be used by God. He will direct you into the area of His will for you by circumstances outside your control, by your successes and failures, and by His Spirit who often influences the desires of your heart. As you learn His direction for your life, you should also be learning in "whatsoever ye do," to "do it heartily, as to the Lord...." (Col. 3:23 KJV)

Second, what is your attitude about the talents that you have been given? The servant who received the two talents did not waste any time or energy complaining about the fact that someone else received more than he did. Neither of the good servants questioned what the master gave them. Rather, they went "at once" and began to work. You, too, should be thankful for the talents you have received. God has trusted you with an amount based upon your "ability" and His wisdom. True, there may be others with more, but there are also others with less. Any talent is a gift from God and it is an opportunity for you to prove to your Master that you are faithful. When you prove your faithfulness, you can know that you will be given greater opportunities. You should also know that you are earning the Master's commendation and you can look forward to sharing His happiness.

Third, what are you doing to multiply your talents? The faithful servants went to work "at once," but the master was gone away "for a long time." Their early enthusiasm from the new opportunity undoubtedly faded and their tasks changed to hard, disciplined work. As more time passed, certainly they were tempted to slack off, but they continued on faithfully. The task of multiplying your athletic talents is not an easy one. It requires sacrifice, discipline, self-denial, and sometimes pain. Multiplying talents is generally difficult, but you have been entrusted with your talents for a purpose, and since that is your calling, you must not "bury" your talent.

Finally, why are you working to multiply your talents? Many athletes are willing to work hard for self-gratification. They are chasing self-esteem, ego-inflation, the feeling of worth, and those brief moments of glory. For most athletes, these are strong motivational factors. However, your motivation as a surrendered Christian athlete is so much greater than that of those athletes. You are working for the commendation of your Creator, the sustainer of the entire universe. You are working for the Lord of lords and the King of kings. You are proving to Him that you are faithful with a few things, so that He will put you in charge of many things. As you work at multiplying your talents, you also need to work at getting to know God better. The better you get to know the Lord, the more you will love Him. The more you love Him, the more you will want to serve and to be faithful to Him. As you grow in your relationship with Him, your motivation to excel will also grow. Your desire to please Him will increase and you will work harder for the day that you will hear the Master say to you, "Well done, good and faithful servant."

Is God pleased with the skills of an excellent athlete? Does He enjoy watching "great athletes" perform? Psalm 147:10 tells us that "He delighteth not in the strength of the horse; He taketh not pleasure in the legs of a man." Your athletic ability and your physical prowess are not what pleases the Lord. His pleasure comes from the faithful efforts of His servant to become all that he can be for the glory of God.

Eric Liddell, the 1924 Olympic 400m Gold medalist who gave his life on the mission field, said, "When I run fast, I feel the Lord's pleasure." Surely God was pleased with what Eric did with his talents and God used his testimony to have a major impact through the movie, *Chariots of Fire*, which was produced long after Eric's death. However, it was not his legs, but his heart that brought God pleasure.

What pleasure are you giving to God? What are you doing with the talents that He has entrusted to you? Go at once. Get to work. Multiply those talents. The Master will return. Will He find you as a faithful servant?

Chapter 4
The Requirement of Sacrifice

Have you ever seen anyone offer a burnt offering? Have you ever offered one yourself? Do you know that the surrendered Christian athlete needs to offer sacrifices? For most of the history of man, sacrifices have been offered upon altars to the true God and to other false gods. The first scriptural reference to such sacrifice is found in Genesis 8. When Noah finally came out of the ark after the flood, he "built an altar to the Lord and, taking some of all the clean animals and clean birds, he sacrificed burnt offerings on it. The Lord smelled the pleasant aroma and said in His heart: 'Never again will I curse the ground because of man, even though every inclination of his heart is evil from childhood. And never again will I destroy all living creatures, as I have done.'" (Gen. 8:20-21 NIV)

The next Biblical reference to sacrifice occurs when "God tested Abraham. God said unto him, "…Take your son, your only son, Isaac, whom you love, and go to the land of Moriah, and offer him there as a burnt offering upon one of the mountains of which I shall tell you.'" (Gen. 22:1-2 RSV) This is the earliest mention of human sacrifice in the Bible. It is likely that Abraham had offered animal sacrifices to God prior to this, for his young son, Isaac, asked him, "My father…Behold the fire and the wood, but where is the lamb for the burnt offering?" Of course, God halted the sacrifice of Isaac, for human sacrifice was contrary to His will, and He supplied a ram for the offering.

Satan has been interested in human sacrifice since the creation of man. Human sacrifice became a common practice among the heathen in the early days. Even today certain Satan worship rituals involve human sacrifice. Many shrines and altars were constructed for the sacrifice of children during the days of the Kings. The abominable practice even reached God's chosen people when King Ahaz of Judah "burnt incense in the valley of the son of Hinnom, and burnt his children in the fire, after the abominations of the heathen whom the Lord had cast out before the children of Israel." (II Chr. 28:3 KJV) King Manasseh, of Judah, also "burnt his sons as an offering in the valley of the son of Hinnom...." (II Chr. 33:6 RSV) This practice was expressly forbidden by God. "There shall not be found among you anyone who burns his son or daughter as an offering." (Deut. 18:10 RSV)

The sacrifice of animals, however, became a requirement of the law in the days of Moses and Aaron. Aaron and his sons were appointed as priests and they alone were given the responsibility of sacrificing the burnt offerings. The Old Testament book of Leviticus deals with the complex regulations that God placed on Israel pertaining to the offering of sacrifices. The requirements were so complex that burnt offerings could not be made correctly without a great deal of knowledge and effort. Properly offered sacrifices made with the right attitude from the people were a "pleasant aroma" to the Lord.

One major requirement for all sacrifices was that the offering to be sacrificed had to be the best the sinner had to offer. An injured or sickly animal was not adequate. Even an average animal was not sufficient. The very best was required. Another requirement of the sacrifice was that the animal was given in its entirety. No part of the animal was returned to be used for food or clothing.

The rituals of sacrifice were ordained by God's laws and were requirements of the Jewish people throughout the Old Testament centuries. Even Jesus' parents followed the Jewish law. "When the time of their purification according to the Law of Moses had been completed, Joseph and Mary took Him [Jesus] to Jerusalem to present Him to the Lord, as it is written in the Law of the Lord, 'Every first born male must be consecrated to the Lord,' and to offer a sacrifice in keeping with what is said in the Law of the Lord, a pair of doves or two young pigeons." (Luke 2:22-24 NIV) According to Leviticus 12, the new mother was required to bring a year-old lamb for a burnt offering, but "if she cannot afford a lamb, she is to bring two doves or two young pigeons." (Lev. 12:8)

The Jewish requirement of sacrifice involving animal death was obeyed to consecrate Jesus, the Lord, to the Lord. However, Jesus, in His perfection, put an end to the requirement of animal sacrifice as He became the perfect human sacrifice that atoned for all sin. "But as it is, He has appeared once for all at the end of the age to put away sin by the sacrifice of Himself. And just as it is appointed for men to die once, and after that comes judgment, so Christ, having been offered once to bear the sins of many, will appear a second time, not to deal with sin but to save those who are eagerly waiting for Him." (Heb. 9:26-28 RSV) "For by a single offering He has perfected for all time those who are sanctified." (Heb. 10:14 RSV)

Christ put an end to sacrifices requiring the shedding of blood and death. Then why is it necessary for us to be involved in sacrifices today? Even after Christ's perfect sacrifice, Paul implores us, "I appeal to you therefore, brethren, by the mercies of God, to present your bodies as a living sacrifice, holy, and acceptable to God, which is your spiritual worship." (Rom. 12:1 RSV) God still desires the sacrifices of His people, but not sacrifices of death. He desires that we present our bodies as living sacrifices. He wants our lives as we live them to be our gifts of worship to Him. "Whatever you do, work at it with all your heart, as working for the Lord...." (Col. 3:23 NIV)

It is not difficult for an athlete to understand the concept of offering his body as a living sacrifice. An athlete sacrifices his body, working with all his heart, in a way that few other workers ever experience. However, offering your efforts as a pleasing sacrifice to your Lord may be even more difficult than offering an Old Testament sacrifice. For your sacrifice to be a "pleasant aroma" to God, your gift to Him must be your absolute best. You begin to realize how difficult this is when you remember that God knows everything about you. If He knows how many hairs are on your head, He also knows what your maximum performance capability is.

Suppose, for example, that you are a runner who is about to compete in the mile. You love the Lord and have decided that you are going to offer your mile race as a sacrifice to Him. You decide that you want to give Him your best, and you would like to also win the race, for Him, of course. As you stand on the starting line, your body is capable of a certain maximum performance. Because of the talents you have received, the training you have done, the rest you have had, the diet you have eaten and the external conditions such as facilities and weather, there is a shortest possible time for you to race this mile. You do not know what that time is but your previous best time is 5:08.5. God knows that on that day you are capable of 5:00.0.

The gun goes off, and one of your competitors dashes into the lead. That athlete sets a pace that feels too fast, but the rest of the field follows. You find yourself in last place after half a lap. Your friends are watching and are cheering for you. You are embarrassed to be in last place when you thought you might win, so you decide to move up and you increase your pace. You pass several runners and come through one lap in the middle of the pack at seventy seconds. Hearing your split time, you know that you are running too fast. You try to relax a little and expect some of the competitors to pass you. No one does and you feel the pace of the race slowing. You know it is too early to push any harder, so you stay in the pack. Friends and family are yelling for you to pass, but your body is telling your mind that passing wouldn't be wise. You pass two laps still right in the middle of the pack at 2:28. You are not happy about that seventy-eight-second lap time. You begin to feel very uncomfortable and though you stay focused and continue to push hard, you can tell that you are slowing even more. The runner just ahead of you is really struggling and you pass him and move into fourth place. You know the third lap is your slowest, but as you hear your three-lap split time of 3:52, revealing an eighty-four-second lap, you move past another runner into third place. Going down the backstretch for the final time you try to find a kick. You are closing on second place and as you go into the final curve, you move into second. Five yards separate you from first place, but your arms and legs are aching and your lungs are burning. You begin to think that second place is pretty good, but then you notice that the gap between you and the lead runner is closing. As you hit the home stretch you are only two yards behind and gaining on the leader. You decide you will win or die trying. You pump your arms as fast as you can and search for your last ounce of energy. Your friends and family are all screaming for you. With thirty yards remaining you pass the leader and sprint across the finish line, exhausted but satisfied. Your last lap took about seventy-eight seconds and your final time is 5:10.2.

Now, if you were offering your race as a sacrifice to your mother, she would say, "Thank you. That was wonderful. First place! I'm sure you did your best." But to God, who sees all things and knows all things, a person whom He knows is capable of a 5:00 mile is giving Him a 5:10.2 and calling it his best. You may argue, "I finished exhausted. I had nothing left. I gave all I had to give." Yet, the question remains, "Was it your best?" "Under the circumstances," you continue, "it was the best I could do. I ran the last half lap as fast as I could. The early pace was just too fast, and I was even in last place for a little while. But, I won the race."

You must recognize, however, that it was your ego that forced you to run faster than you knew you should have on that first lap. If you were truly offering the race as a sacrifice to God, it would be entirely for Him and not at all for yourself. Your ego would not be involved. You would not be at all concerned about what others were thinking of you but would be totally focused on giving and doing your best for the Lord. If you had done that, you may have fallen way behind early and briefly looked like you were not going to be competitive in the race, but you could have caught the leader before three laps and gone on to win by over ten seconds. In other words, you could have done your best.

This is not to say that everything that you do in life must be perfect. However, that which you offer to a Holy God as a sacrificial gift must be from your "first fruits," the best you have to offer.

Imagine, again, that you are a high school basketball player. You are not a starter but usually you are the third or fourth substitute to go into the game. You are involved in a big game tonight with the cross-town rival team, and you decide that you want to offer your efforts as a sacrifice to the Lord. Before the game, you get alone with the Lord and tell Him that you are playing for Him and you are offering the game up to Him.

Your seasonal scoring average is four points per game and you usually see about ten minutes of playing time. Tonight the game is very close and very exciting. There are over twenty lead changes in the game. The coach puts you in for five minutes of the third quarter and you score two points on one-of-three shooting. You play as hard as you know how to, but the coach takes you out when you are called for a second personal foul, one which, in fact, you did not commit. Though it was a bad call by the official, the player you 'fouled' sinks both shots. To make matters worse, your team ends up losing by one point.

After the game you talk to the Lord. "That was a pretty sorry game I gave you. We would have won if the ref hadn't made that bad call on me. I never touched him. We got ripped off. We deserved to win. Coach should have kept me in longer too. I guess I didn't give you much of an offering, did I Lord?"

Your effort in the game may have been your best, but your attitude about the way the game turned out is contaminating your offering. God knows the coach only played you five minutes and He knows why. He knows that you did not commit the second foul that was called on you. He knows if your team deserved to win or not. You must not concern yourself with all the things that are outside of your control. God is in control. When things don't work out the way you want them to, you must accept and respect God's authority and sovereignty and give thanks in all things. You are not responsible for what you cannot control. If you really sacrifice your effort to God, you must not pollute the sacrifice with a sour attitude.

Satan does not like to see you offer a pleasing sacrifice to God, and he will work hard to taint your offering. He has many ways to attempt to ruin your sacrifices. One of his best weapons for destroying our sacrifices is the human ego. It is the biggest element that draws people into athletics and it is the greatest motivational factor for most athletes. We must remember, however, that when a sacrifice was offered in the days of old, the entire animal was given. The sacrifice was completely burned to ashes on the altar. There was nothing left for the one bringing the offering. When you try to receive some glory for an athletic accomplishment, whether before, during, or after the feat, you are taking back something that you have already given to God. The glory should all go to Him.

Satan will also try to keep you from giving your best by distracting or discouraging you. If you lose your focus, you will not be able to offer your very best. He can use all types of conditions to ruin your focus, your performance, and therefore your gift. On a windy day, one athlete competing in the pole vault may be capable of seventeen feet with the wind at his back but only sixteen feet if vaulting into the wind. If the competition is run into the wind, an offering of a sixteen foot vault would be his best, but most athletes would lose their focus under such conditions and would spend too much time thinking about how well they could do if they were jumping in the other direction. It is easy to forget who controls the wind and it is hard to accept that the best possible performance on that day may be far less than what was done in the past. God doesn't measure your performance by the competition or your previous best, but by what He knows you can do on that day. He only desires your best.

Finally, Satan can also taint what is your best effort by contaminating your attitude. He can get you to measure your gift to God by some standard that will make it look bad or good. If it looks bad, you may feel remorse or disgust. If it looks good, you may become proud or self-confident. Offering a pleasing sacrifice to the Lord is not easy, but this should be the goal of every Christian including the Christian athlete. You should not just choose an athletic performance now and then, but you should learn to offer everything to Him. All your performances, all your practices, even all other areas of effort in your life should become sacrifices to Him. That is what it means to "present your body as a living sacrifice" to Him. Learning to do this will result in a blessing on your performances and a blessing on your life.

Imagine that you are about to perform in your area of athletic ability, and you can enter either of two arenas to compete. In one arena, 100,000 sports fans are eagerly waiting to watch the competition. In the other stadium is one man, Jesus Christ, the Son of God, the Creator of the universe, the Lover and Redeemer of your soul. He is sitting there as a man, in the flesh. Which stadium would you enter? Which spectators would motivate you to your best performance?

You may never have the opportunity to compete before 100,000 avid fans, but you do have the opportunity to perform for Jesus Christ. He watches you every day. He sits at the right hand of God making intercession for you, asking the Father to forgive you when "you know not what you do." He loves you. He died for you. He desires and deserves your best. Will you give it to Him?

Chapter 5
The Necessity of Obedience

He was "a coach's dream." He stood head and shoulders above anyone else around, but despite his exceptional height, he was well built. He surely would have had a future in the NBA, but there was no NBA. As if his impressive physical stature was not enough, he was also the most handsome man in all of Israel. Yet, despite all these physical positives, Saul was not a very confident young man. With such an amazing body, Saul might have been proud, but his genuine humility was a pleasant surprise. When the prophet, Samuel, first spoke to him and said, " 'And for whom is all that is desirable in Israel? Is it not for you and your father's house?' Saul answered, 'Am I not a Benjamite, from the least of the tribes of Israel? And is not my family the humblest of all the families of the tribes of Benjamin? Why then have you spoken to me in this way?'" (I Samuel 9:20-21 RSV)

A short time later, after Samuel had anointed Saul to be king of Israel, Saul's uncle asked him what Samuel had said to him, but Saul only told some of what Samuel had said, mentioning nothing about being anointed as the first King of Israel. When a short time later he was chosen by lot to be crowned King of Israel, he could not be found, for he was hiding among some baggage. However, when the Spirit of the Lord came upon him, Saul started ruling as a powerful king. He remained humble and relied on the Lord. With the Lord's blessing he defeated the enemies of Israel and remained obedient to God for two years. Then Saul became confident and began to focus on himself and to disobey God. In I Samuel 15 it is recorded that Samuel said to Saul, "The Lord of hosts says, 'I have in mind what Amalek did to Israel: how he waylaid him when he came up from Egypt. Now then, you go and strike down Amalek; destroy all he has; spare none. Slay man and woman, child and infant, cattle and sheep, camel and donkey.'" (I Samuel 15:2-3 ML) Then "Saul struck down Amalek from Havilah to the Shur approach east of Egypt. He captured Agag, the Amalek king, alive, but he doomed all the people to complete destruction with the sword. However, Saul and the people spared Agag; also, the choicest sheep and cattle and the fattest lambs—everything of high value they did not doom to destruction; only the lesser quality cattle and the worthless they utterly destroyed." (I Samuel 15:7-9 ML)

The Lord told Samuel about Saul's sin of disobedience, but when Samuel went looking for Saul, he did not find him because Saul had left to "erect a monument for himself." His humility was gone. When Samuel caught up with Saul, "Saul said, 'The Lord bless you. I have carried out the Lord's command.' But Samuel said, 'What then is this bleating of sheep and lowing of cattle that I hear?' Saul replied, 'They have brought them along from the Amalekites; the people have spared the best of the sheep and cattle to bring an offering to the Lord your God, but the rest we have destroyed.' Samuel then said to Saul.…'When you were little in your own sight, did you not become a prince of Israel's tribes, and has not the Lord anointed you to be king over Israel? The Lord sent you out under orders. He said: Go and destroy the evildoers, the Amalekites; fight them until you have exterminated them. Why then did you not listen to the Lord's voice, but flung yourself on the loot and did evil in the Lord's sight?' Saul answered Samuel, 'I did listen to the Lord's voice and went the way the Lord sent me. I brought along Agag, the Amalekite king, and I have doomed the Amalekites to destruction; but the people took of the choicest sheep and cattle, the best that was doomed, to bring sacrifices to the Lord your God at Gilgal.' Samuel then said, 'Does the Lord delight as much in burnt offerings and in sacrifices as in obeying the Lord's voice? See! Obedience is better than sacrifice and to listen (is better) than the fat of rams. For rebellion is as the sin of fortune telling and stubbornness as wickedness and idol worship. Because you have rejected the Lord's word, He has rejected you from being King.'" (I Samuel 15:13-23 ML)

Saul's argument sounds rather convincing. He claimed that he saved the best of the cattle and sheep for an offering to the Lord. Wasn't that the kind of offering that the Lord desired, the very best? The reasoning may sound logical for "every way of man is right in his own eyes, but the Lord weighs the heart. To do righteousness and justice is more acceptable to the Lord than sacrifice." (Prov. 21:2-3 RSV) Again in Jeremiah we read, "I will bring evil upon this people...because they have not hearkened unto my words, not to my law, but rejected it. To what purpose cometh there to me incense from Sheba and the sweet cane from a far country? Your burnt offerings are not acceptable, nor your sacrifices sweet unto me." (Jer. 6:19-20 KJV)

Though the Word of God implores you to "present your body as a living sacrifice," the Lord does not desire your gifts and sacrifices if He does not first have your obedience. Meaningful gifts are given as expressions of love and it is our love that the Lord most desires. When Christ was asked what was the most important commandment, He responded "...you shall love the Lord your God with all your heart, and with all your soul, and with all your mind, and with all your strength." (Mark 12:30 RSV) "To love Him with all the heart, and with all the understanding, and with all the strength...is much more than all whole burnt offerings and sacrifices." (Mark 12:33 RSV) In other words, obedience is a better expression of love than sacrifice. Obedience is in fact a sacrifice of the will, a sacrifice of the individual will of the man to the will of God as indicated in His commands. Jesus said, "If a man loves me, he will keep my word...He who does not love me does not keep my words." (John 14:23-24 RSV) God has given us His word, the Holy Word of God, and we must commit ourselves to obeying that word in order to be in a position to offer Him pleasing sacrifices.

Without your obedience, your "offerings are not acceptable, nor your sacrifices sweet unto" Him.

Gwen Torrence was one of the favorites to win gold medals for the USA in the sprints at the 1995 World Championships. She captured the gold in the 100m, edging Jamaica's Merlene Ottey by 0.09 seconds. However, in the 200m it appeared to be no contest as she sprinted to victory in 21.77, a full 0.35 seconds ahead of Merlene in second place. The performance was outstanding considering the 2.2-meter per second head wind. She, the crowd, and even the television commentators celebrated her victory until the announcement came that she had been disqualified. She had stepped on the inside lane line running around the curve. The rulebook reads, "Disqualification shall be ruled when a competitor steps on or over the lane line to the left on a curve with two consecutive steps of the left foot." The fact that she won by 0.35 seconds and probably gained less than 0.1 second of advantage by the infraction did not matter. The rule violation did not move her back to second or third place, but disqualified her. The result was the same as if she had not run the race at all. Without obedience to the rules of competition, the effort she sacrificed was of no value. Merlene Ottey, who has been known as the Bronze Queen for all the bronze medals she had won through her long career, came away with the gold medal. The same is true in almost all sports. The basket scored after a traveling violation does not count. The touchdown scored following a clipping action is called back. Play must be done according to the rules, or the benefits are not awarded.

The Word of God is full of commandments and laws. It is a guidebook of directions for our lives. How can we know and obey them all? What areas of obedience are required to be able to offer a pleasing sacrifice? Where should we begin to live a life of obedience? Jesus summarized the whole law in two commands—to love God above all else and to love your neighbor as yourself. These commands are the basis for every other command in the Bible. Loving God above all else will enable you to obey God's commands related to worship, to idolatry, and to revering God's name. Loving your neighbor as yourself prepares you to obey God's commands pertaining to your treatment of your parents, your brothers and sisters, your neighbor, the unknown man on the street, and even your enemies. True love for all other humans, humans that God loves, will put an end to lying, stealing, cheating, adultery, fornication, covetousness, and murder. It is the basis for right relationships with all of mankind. Your heart must be right not only with God but also with other men before you are able to offer a pleasing sacrifice to the Lord. Jesus said, "So if you are offering your gift at the altar, and there remember that your brother has something against you, leave your gift there before the altar and go; first be reconciled to your brother, and then come and offer your gift." (Matt. 5:23-24 RSV)

Learning true obedience to God is a lifetime process, but it begins with the right attitude of the heart. When you are disobedient, you must confess your sin and be cleansed by the blood of Christ, which He offered as a sacrifice to pay the penalty for all your sins. Before your confession, you can say with the Psalmist, "Thou hast no delight in sacrifice; were I to give it, Thou wouldst not be pleased. The sacrifice acceptable to God is a broken spirit; a broken and contrite heart, O God, Thou wilt not despise...then, wilt Thou delight in right sacrifices.... (Ps. 51: 16-17, 19 RSV) When your heart is "broken and contrite," when you have confessed and turned from your sin and are in a position of obedience to God, then you can in love offer your best to Him, and that offering will bring pleasure to the Almighty God. What a wonderful, humbling, and amazing thought this is, that you as a mere mortal, a human in the flesh, seemingly insignificant in this world, can bring pleasure to the Almighty Creator. Shouldn't you desire to do that more than anything else? Do you?

Chapter 6
The Poison of Pride

Davivid was a great athlete. A study of his life reveals that. Though certainly not of the physical stature of Saul, he was nevertheless powerful for his size. However, it was his quickness, his agility, and his movement skills that helped make him an exceptional athlete and warrior. When Saul, without warning, twice hurled his spear at David from close range, it was his outstanding athleticism that saved his life. If Saul would have made an impressive center on a basketball team, David would have been a tremendous guard. Yet, more than his athletic skills, it was his heart that really made David such a great athlete. This is not surprising, for the Bible calls him a man after God's own heart. (I Sam. 13:14) When as a shepherd boy he was tending his father's sheep and a lion grabbed one of the sheep, David did not show any fear but grabbed the lion by the beard and slew him. He did the exact same thing with a bear, giving no thought to his own well being. Was that why David had no fear of Goliath? If you had to fight a lion, a bear, or a nine-foot tall giant to the death, which one would you choose?

Any coach would love to have just one athlete on his team with such great heart, an athlete who showed such courage and confidence in the face of seemingly unbeatable competition. In his battles with animals, David reacted as an athlete with a big heart. He had little time to contemplate his actions or to be discouraged by the gravity of the situation. However, in the competition with Goliath, things were different. When he saw Goliath mocking the armies of Israel, he had time to think about his actions. When he began asking questions and showing some interest in volunteering to fight Goliath, his oldest brother became angry with him and accused him of being proud and cocky. When he was brought to King Saul, even King Saul said, "Don't be ridiculous. How can a kid like you fight with a man like him?" (I Sam. 17:33 TLB) But none of these things discouraged David. When Saul put his own armor on David, David could hardly move in it. Goliath himself wore a coat of mail that weighed two hundred pounds. Yet, none of these discouraging facts did anything to deter the confidence of David, because his confidence was not in himself. David was not cocky. On the contrary, he had tremendous confidence in God and that confidence was exhibited in his words to Goliath, "You come to me with a sword and with a spear and with a javelin; but I come to you in the name of the Lord of hosts, the God of the armies of Israel, whom you have defied. This day the Lord will deliver you into my hand, and I will strike you down and cut off your head; and I will give the dead bodies of the host of the Philistines this day to the birds of the air and to the wild beasts of the earth, that all the earth may know that there is a God in Israel, and that all this assembly may know that the Lord saves not with sword or spear; for the battle is the Lord's and He will give you into our hand." (I Sam. 17:45-47 NIV)

How could David be so sure that God would give him victory on that day? How did he know that Goliath's incredible power would not over-power him? David knew with a certainty that Goliath would not kill him because God's prophet, Samuel, had anointed David to be king. If God had chosen David to be the next king of Israel, God would not allow him to be killed. In addition to that knowledge, the Spirit of the Lord had come upon him after he was anointed by Samuel. This was the same Spirit that lives in Christians today. That Holy Spirit could communicate with David's spirit so that David could know things that no human had told him. We will look at this phenomenon more closely in chapter 13, The Will of God— The Voice of the Spirit.

David certainly had a close relationship with God and knew God well. A study of the Psalms that David wrote in his early life shows that he, as a young man, already had a very close relationship with the Lord.

Yet, in spite of this relationship and the mighty way that God blessed and used David, David still struggled with sin. If asked, "What was David's sin?" almost everyone would have an answer even in this day of widespread Biblical ignorance. Most would say that his sin was adultery with Bathsheba and some would add that his sin was the murder of Uriah. If we measure the severity of a sin by God's penalty for committing it, we would say that indeed the situation with Bathsheba was a serious sin. The prophet Nathan told David, "The sword will never depart from your house, because you despised me and took the wife of Uriah the Hittite to be your own. This is what the Lord says, 'Out of your own household I am going to bring calamity upon you. Before your very eyes I will take your wives and give them to one who is close to you, and he will lie with your wives in broad daylight. You did it in secret, but I will do it in broad daylight, before all Israel.'" Then David said to Nathan, "I have sinned against the Lord." Nathan replied, "The Lord has taken away your sin. You are not going to die. But because by doing this you have made the enemies of the Lord show utter contempt, the son born to you will die." (II Sam. 12:10-14) David and Bathsheba's son did die seven days after his birth, and David's son, Absalom, later in David's life "pitched a tent... on the roof, and he lay with his father's concubines in the sight of all Israel." (II Sam. 16:22 NIV) Absalom also was later murdered. How many other of the descendants of David died by the "sword that did not depart from his house" as a result of David's sin is not known, but it may have been dozens or even more.

Though this serious sin of David is most well known, David committed another sin, a sin that was punished with the deaths of 70,000 people. What terrible sin did he commit that resulted in such a serious punishment? If less than one hundred people died from his sin involving Bathsheba, what sin could be so serious that it would warrant the deaths of probably over seven hundred times that many people? That terrible sin was the sin of pride.

You may be thinking, "David was not a proud man." In fact, there were several instances in his life that showed humility. When he was at the cave of Adullam pining for a "drink of water from the well near the gate of Bethlehem," (I Chr. 11:17) unknown to him three of his mighty men broke through the Philistine lines risking their lives to bring him that water. A proud man would have been pleased and honored that he was held in such high esteem that his men would risk their lives just to bring him a drink of water. He would have thought how important he was. But David "refused to drink it; instead, he poured it out before the Lord. 'God forbid that I should do this!' he said. 'Should I drink the blood of these men who went at the risk of their lives?' Because they risked their lives to bring it back, David would not drink it." (I Chr. 11:18-19) Such actions were not indicative of a man who struggled against pride. However, pride is a poison that can show up at any time, especially when God is blessing and things are going well. That is what happened to David.

There came a time in David's reign as king when things were going very well. His armies defeated the Ammonites and the Philistines and David began to feel good about the power of his kingdom and Israel's army. Then "Satan rose up against Israel and incited David to take a census of Israel. So David said to Joab and the commanders of the troops, 'Go and count the Israelites from Beersheba to Dan. Then report back to me so that I may know how many there are.' But Joab recognized the sin in this desire and replied, 'May the Lord multiply his troops a hundred times over. My lord the king, are they not all my lord's subjects? Why does my lord want to do this? Why should he bring guilt on Israel?' The king's word, however, overruled Joab; so Joab left and went throughout Israel and then came back to Jerusalem. Joab reported the number of the fighting men to David: In all Israel there were one million, one hundred thousand men who could handle a sword, including four hundred and seventy thousand in Judah." (I Chr. 21:1-5 NIV)

This command of David was "evil in the sight of God; so He punished Israel." (I Chr. 21:7) The Lord sent a prophet to David to offer him a choice of three punishments—three years of famine, three months of being overrun by Israel's enemies, or three days of plague. David chose the third option because he said he would rather fall into the hands of the Lord whose mercy is very great rather than fall into the hands of men. Then the angel of the Lord slew 70,000 men of Israel and was ready to slay more. "David looked up and saw the angel of the Lord standing between heaven and earth, with a drawn sword in his hand extended over Jerusalem. Then David and the elders, clothed in sackcloth, fell face down. David said to God, 'Was it not I who ordered the fighting men to be counted? I am the one who has sinned and done wrong. These are but sheep. What have they done? O Lord my God, let your hand fall upon me and my family, but do not let this plague remain on your people.'" (I Chr. 21:16-17 NIV) Then God commanded the angel and he returned his sword to its sheath.

Many of us would not recognize the sin in David's order to count his troops. Why is this such a terrible sin that God would require such a severe punishment? Recall that in David's battle with Goliath, David did not rely on the strength of Israel's army. He did not rely on armor and, in fact, went into battle without any. He did not even trust his skill with a sling and a stone. He knew that God would deliver him and he trusted only God. Years later, when David was a successful king, Satan started him thinking about the size and power of his army, as if the army was the security of Israel. He became proud of the size of the army that he commanded. David should have remembered that Israel's only security was in God and there was no reason to give any attention to the size of the army. Joab recognized the king's order as sin, but pride makes it very difficult to accept wise counsel. Pride makes us trust in our own abilities. It is a poison that can kill our relationship with God. God's desire is that His children go through life, led by the Spirit, trusting in God, and doing His will. When pride creeps in, God is pushed off the throne, self is placed on the throne, and the child's relationship with the Father is destroyed.

God hates the sin of pride. "Everyone who is arrogant is an abomination to the Lord; be assured, he will not go unpunished." (Pr. 16:5 RSV) The first thing listed among the "six things the Lord hates, seven that are detestable to him" (Pr. 6:16) is haughty eyes or a proud look. Even before a proud word is spoken or a proud deed is done, God sees the proud look and hates it. Therefore the Bible tells us that God delivers "the humble but condemns the proud and haughty ones." (Ps. 18:27 TLB) It was the sin of pride that God punished when He confused men's languages at the tower of Babel, for men said, "Come, let us build ourselves a city, and a tower with its top in the heavens, and let us make a name for ourselves..." (Gen. 11:4 RSV) This is the same attitude that motivates so many people (especially athletes) today. "Let me make a name for myself." Take a few moments and reflect upon this. How much of your motivation in your athletics has been to make a name for yourself, to be someone that other people consider important? How much of your present motivation is to achieve adulation for yourself? In Jeremiah we read, "Thus says the Lord: Let not the wise man boast in his wisdom, let not the mighty man boast in his strength, let not the rich man boast in his riches; but let the one who glories boast in this, that he understands and knows Me, that I am the Lord who practices loving-kindness, justice, and righteousness in the earth; for in these things I delight, says the Lord." (Jer. 9:23-24 ML)

If this sin grieved God in Old Testament days, how much more must it grieve Him in the New Testament Age when His children, children whom He has adopted through the sacrificial death of His Son, are still motivated by pride. We should be able to say with Paul, "I have been crucified with Christ; it is no longer I who live, but Christ who lives in me...." (Gal. 2:20 RSV) If you have died to self, how can you be motivated to glorify self? "Our old self was crucified with Him so that the sinful body might be destroyed, and we might no longer be enslaved to sin. For he who has died is freed from sin." (Rom. 6:6-7 RSV) Dying to self is the challenge of the Christian life. It is difficult, but it is necessary if you are going to live for Christ. You must learn to "do nothing from selfishness or conceit, but in humility count others better than yourself. Let each of you look not only to his own interests, but also to the interests of others." (Phil. 2:3-4 RSV) Paul learned this self-denial, for he said, "I consider my life worth nothing to me, if only I may finish the race and complete the task the Lord Jesus has given me.... (Acts 20:24 NIV) He also said, "May I never boast except in the cross of our Lord Jesus Christ, through which the world has been crucified to me, and I to the world." (Gal 5:14 RSV) "If anyone is going to boast, let him boast only of what the Lord has done." (I Cor. 1:31 TLB)

When the Holy Spirit is in control of your life, there is no place for pride. "If we live by the Spirit, let us also walk by the Spirit. Let us have no self-conceit, no provoking of one another, no envying of one another." (Gal. 5:25-26 RSV) When God is on the throne of your life, you will not only avoid pride about your strengths, but you will also learn contentment in your weaknesses. His grace will prove sufficient for you, for His power is made perfect in weakness. As Paul said, "I will all the more gladly boast of my weaknesses, that the power of Christ may rest upon me. For the sake of Christ, then, I am content with weakness, insults, hardship, persecutions, and calamities; for when I am weak, then I am strong." (II Cor. 12:9-10 RSV)

From my first phone conversation with John I sensed that he was like David, a man after God's own heart. Though he failed to tell me exactly what his previous athletic accomplishments were, I learned enough to believe that he would be an asset to our team. He dropped the names of several high level athletes with whom he had worked and told me about how he came to know the Lord. Because he obviously loved the Lord and because he was also very interested in competing for a Division I track team, he quickly developed a strong interest in our program at Liberty University. John considered himself to be primarily a triple jumper but he also was collegiate competitive in the long jump. He might even be able and willing to fill in on a sprint relay leg if needed, but in his mind he was first and foremost a triple jumper. Based upon the impact that we felt he could have, we offered John a partial athletic scholarship. That made it possible for him to join us. Since he had attended another college a few years earlier, he only had two years of eligibility when he arrived at Liberty.

Right from the beginning John was at home at Liberty. He loved the spiritually enriching environment, the many Christian friendships that he developed, his Christian professors, and the abundance of spiritual growth activities that are such a major part of life at Liberty. He quickly became a spiritual leader on the track team and displayed a depth of Biblical knowledge and spiritual maturity beyond that of the typical Liberty student. He was not afraid of hard work, but it soon became apparent that he had a somewhat independent mind when it came to training. He began to adjust his workouts from that which was prescribed to what he felt he should do. However, John was so heavenly minded that I did not worry about him at all. If all our team members were like him, I would have been happy. I didn't give any consideration to the fact that there might be a serious problem.

The first competitive triple jump I remember seeing him execute was well beyond our school record, but he fouled it slightly and therefore it did not count and was not measured. I was nevertheless pleased because I was confident that he would soon break the record and become an impact athlete on our team. However, the good performances that I expected never came. There always seemed to be some problem that prevented the success that everyone expected. As the season progressed, he battled injuries and other unusual misfortunes amidst a growing desire to prove himself. When his first year at Liberty ended, he had accomplished very little in athletics.

There have been times when I have seen Christian athletes struggle for a while but then, "in due season, they reap if they faint not." That is what I expected for John. His final season would be the reward for which he had worked and waited. That is what I believed and expected. However, I was wrong. John's final collegiate season continued to be a constant struggle and the indoor season passed without a performance that brought any satisfaction to him or the coaches. When the team went on the spring break trip to Florida, who should we find training at the same facility with our team but another Jon, Jonathan Edwards, the world record holder in the triple jump and an outspoken Christian athlete. John seemed to be in heaven. He took every opportunity to talk with Jonathan and he seemed incredibly enamoured with him. He got some pointers from the world record holder and was tremendously motivated to jump well at that meet. Despite an abundance of motivation, the results did not come.

John continued to struggle and did not qualify for the Penn Relays in either of his specialties, but when one of our sprinters sustained an injury, we needed a fourth man for our 4x100m relay. We decided to bring John to run the second leg. In the trial round, the team did well enough to advance to a final. In the final race, John received the baton in his hand near the wrong end of the baton and he didn't have the experience to adjust it. When he tried to hand it to the third runner, there was too little of the stick exposed and the baton dropped to the track. John had to face yet another disappointment and to share that with his irritated teammates.

Because of John's heart for the Lord and spiritual maturity, it had not even occurred to me that John's problem might be a spiritual problem. As I reflected upon his athletic history at Liberty, something began to become clear to me. I realized that he idolized high level athletes. He also had a way, without lying, of leading others to believe that he had accomplished more than he actually had. He so badly desired athletic success. It also was apparent that he wanted others to know that he was a high level athlete. As I reflected upon his situation, I counted seven symptoms that led me to believe that John was ingesting the poison of pride.

Certainly John was not unique in this. Many athletes are greatly motivated by their pride and the Lord still allows them to have outstanding athletic success. There have also been other leaders who have counted their soldiers without direct punishment from God. But David was a man after God's own heart, and therefore God was particularly distressed when that heart became filled with pride. David had been richly blessed by God because God, not self, had been on the throne of David's life. Just as God would not allow that pride to go unpunished in David's heart, so too, I believe, God wanted John's heart completely, and He would do whatever it took to get John to surrender this part of himself, his pride, into God's hands.

When I called John into my office, he came with the emotions that grew out of the athletic frustration that he had experienced for nearly two years. It was difficult to tell a godly young man that I believed he had a serious problem with pride. Who was I to tell him that? How much of my drive to see our team succeed was motivated by my own desire to be known as a good coach? Would I be trying to get the moat out of his eye when I couldn't see clearly because of the beam in my own eye? Regardless of these thoughts, I felt it was my duty, and so I revealed to him what I believed was his real problem.

I am not sure if I offended him at first or not, but he listened intently and prayerfully reflected upon these things in the coming days. Seeing your own pride can be a difficult task, but John confessed it and began to work at eliminating it. His athletic performances finally began to improve and he qualified for our major championship meet in both the triple jump and long jump. He even ran a few 100m races and ran a personal best of 10.81, not as good as three of the sprinters on our 4x100m relay, but about the same as the other long jumper who sometimes ran the relay. The week before the championship meet he had some problems with cramping leg muscles, but we made the decision to run John on the relay if he felt able to go. We made the decision to run him as the anchor leg on the relay so that it would not matter if he got the baton in his hand in the wrong place because he would not have to hand it off. Since he was our slowest runner on the relay, a handoff deep in the zone would also mean that he could run the shortest distance.

This meet, the 1996 IC4A championship, was very important to us since we had set the goal to win the meet. Over seventy teams were represented, including the indoor national champions from that year. The 4x100m trials went very well, with our team easily winning their heat in a school record, 39.86. However, in another heat the defending meet champions clocked 39.72. They, therefore, had lane four in the final with our team in lane five. When they had a bad handoff on the first exchange, the Liberty team opened up a lead that grew to about three or four meters by the end of the second turn. John took the baton with this lead, and it quickly became evident that he was no match for the anchorman chasing him. Within fifty-meters, three quarters of the lead had disappeared and it seemed certain that John would be passed. However, as they neared the finish line, the gap began to close much more slowly, and at the finish line it was a photo finish. John leaned at the line and that lean gave his team a victory by 0.01 seconds, 40.22 to 40.23. The result produced a swing in the score of four points, which in the end proved to be the difference for the Liberty team.

God used a moment when John was being caught from behind, potentially being embarrassed by another sprinter, when he was doing what he didn't do best and what he didn't think was his athletic gift, to be his greatest moment. John contributed to the greatest upset victory in Liberty track history and perhaps the greatest in

Liberty sports history, but not in the way that he always imagined he would. In the midst of a humbling experience, God allowed John to have a major impact in the collegiate track world. God will certainly use anyone "whose heart is perfect toward Him," but if the heart is perfect toward Him, it will not tell God what to do. That person will be available to God to be used however God chooses, not harboring any selfish ambition.

The pride of life is one of the greatest areas of failure for Christian athletes. Much spiritual wisdom is required to recognize and resist temptations on this front. "Who is wise and understanding among you? Let him show it by his good life, by deeds done in the **humility that comes from wisdom.** But if you harbor bitter envy and selfish ambition in your hearts, do not boast about it or deny the truth. Such 'wisdom' does not come down from heaven, but is earthly, unspiritual, of the devil. For where you have envy and selfish ambition, there you find disorder and every evil practice. But the wisdom that comes from heaven is first of all pure; then peace loving, considerate, submissive, full of mercy and good fruit, impartial and sincere. Peacemakers who sow in peace raise a harvest of righteousness." (James 3:13-17 NIV) James is very clear about the source of selfish ambition. He says it is "of the devil."

By accepting Jesus Christ as Savior, a man will in a moment possess the Spirit of God, but he does not immediately possess spiritual wisdom. It takes time to develop this important quality. For this reason, Paul exhorts Timothy to bypass new Christians when choosing church leaders. "He must not be a recent convert, or he may become conceited and fall under the same judgment as the devil." (I Tim. 3:6 NIV) However, Christian athletes are not generally chosen from the spiritually mature. Athletic prowess is usually a gift given to the young, so there is an increased danger that the human inclination toward pride and self-centeredness will overcome the Christian athlete. Coaches, teammates, sportswriters, fans, and sometimes even competitors often treat a successful athlete as if he were very special. It is not difficult for an athlete to develop celebrity status within at least a small group of admirers through athletic accomplishment. As an athlete encounters more success, it becomes increasingly difficult to avoid the pitfalls of pride amidst the adulation of increasing numbers.

As a result, the blessing of God is often followed by the sin of pride. We have already seen this in the life of King David. King Uzziah and King Hezekiah were "good" kings of Judah who also became victims of this sin. "As long as the king (Uzziah) followed the paths of God, he prospered, for God blessed him." (II Chr. 26:5b TLB) He won many victories and amassed great wealth. "So he became very famous, for the Lord helped him wonderfully until he was very powerful. But at that point he became proud—and corrupt. He sinned against the Lord his God by entering the forbidden sanctuary of the temple and personally burning incense upon the altar." (II Chr. 26:15b-16 TLB) For this sin, Uzziah was struck with leprosy, which remained with him the rest of his life.

King Hezekiah spent much of his reign cleansing the temple and returning Israel to the religious customs that she had abandoned. When he was besieged by a huge Assyrian army, he prayed for deliverance and the Lord sent His angel to destroy the Assyrians. Hezekiah won a great victory without even engaging in a single battle. "From then on, Hezekiah became immensely respected among the surrounding nations, and many gifts for the Lord arrived at Jerusalem, with valuable presents for King Hezekiah too. But about that time, Hezekiah became deathly sick, and he prayed to the Lord, and the Lord replied with a miracle. However, Hezekiah didn't respond with true thanksgiving and praise, for he had become proud and so the anger of God was upon him." (II Chr. 32:24-25 TLB)

When you accepted Jesus Christ as your savior, God began an important work within you, the work of conforming you to the image of Jesus Christ. You can be confident "that He who began a good work in you will bring it to completion at the day of Jesus

Christ." (Phil. 1:6 RSV) God wants to bless you and to use you, but it is even more important to Him to conform you to Jesus Christ. If God blesses you in your athletic endeavors, and that blessing begins to cause you to become proud, you can expect that God will remove that blessing from you. "Before his downfall a man's heart is proud, but humility comes before honor." (Prov. 18:12 NIV) Paul exhorts every Christian "not to think of himself more highly than he ought to think, but to think with sober judgment, each according to the measure of faith which God has assigned him." (Rom. 12:3 RSV)

If God places His hand of blessing upon your athletics, how much success will you be able to withstand before you begin to think too highly of yourself? How many articles that extol your tremendous performances can you read before you start to believe them? How many victories can you orchestrate before you begin to think that you are better than others?

A master craftsman, musician and composer had two old blocks of wood. He took one, and with great skill and care fashioned a magnificent violin. From the other block he made a violin stand. He placed the violin on the stand. One evening he took the violin and went to play a concert. With unmatched skill he played a series of original compositions that amazed and delighted all those who heard. Later that evening he placed the violin back on the stand. The violin said to the stand, "You should have seen and heard what I did tonight. Thousands of people gave me applause like you will never know. I was fantastic."

Obviously this personified violin has no grounds for pride. An attitude of pride is foolish and sinful. It is foolish because it involves forgetting what we really are. "The greatest of men, or the lowest—both alike are nothing...." (Ps. 62:9a TLB) It is sinful because it involves forgetting who God really is, and what He has done. "My protection and success come from God alone." (Ps. 62:7a TLB) We can easily recognize that except for the will and skill of the master, both the violin and the stand are nothing but old blocks of wood, which he could choose to use for firewood if he willed. Though this is easy to see in this example, it is difficult for us to remember what we are except for the work and skill of the Master. We are but dust. We should be grateful for the labor that God has invested in us and to honor Him should be our whole purpose. As Jesus said, "He who speaks on his own does so to gain honor for himself, but he who works for the honor of the one who sent him is a man of truth; there is nothing false about him." (John 7:18 NIV) Though Jesus was speaking about himself, as a Christian you also have been sent as God's ambassador to the world, and you also should be working for the honor of the one who sent you.

Pride is a very subtle sin. It can overtake a man or woman with very little warning. It is rarely recognized by the offender and often is not distinguished by others. In many cases it is even encouraged by parents and coaches and is sometimes considered healthy "self-esteem."

Pride evidences itself in several different ways. Yet, in all its forms it is a poison that can kill. It can kill the blessing of God on your efforts. It can destroy your testimony for Christ. It can damage your relationship with God.

The most obvious form of pride is seen in the boaster. This person thinks that he is superior and it is apparent from what he says and how he acts. When he speaks he overuses the words, "I," "me," and "my." In the extreme case he brags about what he has done and what he is going to do. The former boxer, Cassius Clay, who later changed his name to Mohammed Ali, appeared as a classic case. Though such a person is often viewed as obnoxious, many people are attracted by his apparent confidence because it represents something they wish they had.

More frequently, pride is not as evident in a person's words but it does its damage in his mind. The person with this more common strain of pride thinks that he deserves the better things in life. He feels he is entitled to more opportunities, more success, and more honor. He does not like to see others have success. Observing their success only makes him think about himself. He may appear psychologically healthy to everyone and he may even be likable, but his mind is filled with himself. This attitude is very common among athletes.

A third form of pride often appears to be the exact opposite of pride. A person with this condition is considered to have an inferiority complex. He acts humble and says or implies that he is not as good as others. He has an inordinate fear of failure. However, in reality, in most cases he has such a high opinion of himself that he cannot accept his image being tarnished in any way. He would rather bypass activity and opportunity than risk the possibility of failure that comes with it. He will only attempt something if he can be sure of success. Though it is difficult to recognize, his problem is pride. He is focused on himself instead of on God, the Creator who wants to use him.

The temptation toward pride is real to everyone, and certainly to all athletes. Aspiring Christian athletes need to beware of the poison of pride. Hear this warning of the Lord, "I warned the proud to cease their arrogance! I told the wicked to lower their insolent gaze, and to stop being stubborn and proud. For promotion and power come from nowhere on earth, but only from God. He promotes one and deposes another." (Ps. 75:4-7 TLB) "And what does the Lord require of you? To act justly and to love mercy and to walk *humbly* with your God." (Micah 6:8 NIV)

Chapter 7
The Danger of Discouragement

If he thought about it, he could still remember that incredible feeling. He had never run like that before in his life and neither had anyone else. His performance was certainly a world record, but it would never be ratified. In fact, his amazing performance had been observed by only one other human. Yes, if he tried he could remember the feeling of running like the wind, step after step, mile after mile, covering ground with no signs of fatigue. How could this great run have been possible? He had been running before a king, a king who was chasing him in a horse drawn chariot. The king had watched him running just ahead of him, with a terrible storm rising behind him, but though he drove his team hard, the king could not catch the fleet-footed runner. It was not because of his equipment, for he had no Nike Airs, Reebok Pumps or Asics Gels. He ran only in sandals. It was not due to his light running apparel, for he ran with his heavy cloak tucked into his belt. It was not the result of his great training regimen, for he had not trained for the run. It was because the power of the Lord had come upon Elijah.

The wicked King Ahab had watched the power of the Lord on a man running in front of him for the twenty-three miles from Mount Carmel to Jezreel, while at the same time seeing an evidence of God's power behind him as he drove his horses ahead of a terrible storm. That storm had brought the first rain in three and a half years, the first rain that King Ahab had seen since Elijah had told him there would be no dew or rain for the next few years.

However, that world record run had not been Elijah's greatest feat. Just hours earlier he had staged the battle of the gods, Baal with his 450 prophets against the one true living God, with his one prophet, Elijah. The former team had been unable to produce fire from heaven to ignite the bull on their altar, but in front of all Israel, Elijah had prayed and God had answered with His fire from heaven. That fire had consumed Elijah's bull, the wood, the water from twelve barrels that had soaked the sacrifice and even the twelve large stones that made up the altar. At Elijah's command, the Israelites had then seized and killed Baal's 450 prophets. What a great victory that had been! What a powerful instrument Elijah had been in God's hands. It seemed the exhilaration of that experience might have carried Elijah in the early steps of the twenty-three mile run.

But now Elijah sat under a broom tree in the desert, and he was distraught. He was not even thinking of his recent victories, for he was in the depths of discouragement. His prayer to God was, "I have had enough, Lord. Take my life; I am no better than my ancestors." (I Kings 19:4 NIV)

How had Elijah fallen so far in just a matter of days? Was it only Queen Jezebel's threat to take Elijah's life that took him so quickly from the podium of victory to the portals of defeat and the depths of discouragement? How could the man who stood against King Ahab and four hundred prophets of Baal fall at the words of one woman? Was Jezebel such a powerful woman to warrant Elijah's reaction?

No, it was not the change in his circumstances that had Elijah so discouraged. It was, rather, his change in focus. During the events leading up to Elijah's triumph on Mount Carmel, he had been focused on God. A study of these chapters will show that Elijah was only doing what God had told him to do. He was obeying God and believing that God would do what He said He would do. God had even told Elijah that He would send rain again. So when the time was right for the rain, Elijah had prayed and then sent his servant to check the sky for clouds. When there were none, Elijah had prayed again, and again sent his servant away. He had done this six times, and each time his servant had returned, seeing nothing in the sky.

Yet, Elijah had not been discouraged, for his faith in God was strong and his eyes were on what God was doing. Elijah had prayed a seventh time and that time his servant had reported that he saw a small cloud. Then Elijah, knowing the rain was coming soon, had "girded up his loins" and had begun to run.

Now, however, his focus was not on God. Hear his words again, "I have had enough, Lord. Take my life; I am no better than my ancestors." Two "I's" and two "my's" in just fifteen words. Compare that with his prayer on Mount Carmel. "Oh Lord, God of Abraham, Isaac and Israel, let it be known today that you are God in Israel and that I am your servant and have done all these things at your command." We read three direct references to God, two "yours" and one "you" in just thirty-four words. Elijah's focus had clearly shifted from God and what He was doing to himself and what he was feeling. Instead of seeing God's power, he was seeing his own weakness. Instead of looking at who he was in God, he saw who he was in himself. So, naturally, he was very discouraged. Without food or water, he laid down in the desert to die, and fell asleep.

Then the Angel of the Lord awakened him and told him to get up and eat. Elijah got up and ate a cake of bread and drank a jar of water the angel had prepared for him. He was revived physically but not encouraged, for he lay down again. A second time the angel touched him and said, "Get up and eat, for the journey is too much for you." After eating and drinking the second time, Elijah was physically strengthened to the point that he traveled forty days and forty nights in the desert on the strength that he gained from the food prepared by the angel. However, he was still focused upon himself and was deeply discouraged. He accomplished nothing for the Lord during that time. Like the Israelites who wandered forty years in that same wilderness, missing out on God's blessings in the Promised Land because of their discouragement, Elijah was missing what God had planned for him because of his discouragement. After forty days he arrived at a cave at Mount Horeb "and the word of the Lord came to him asking, 'What are you doing here, Elijah?' He replied, 'I have been very zealous for the Lord God Almighty. The Israelites have rejected your covenant, broken down your altars, and put your prophets to death with the sword. I am the only one left, and now they are trying to kill me too.'" (I Kings 19:9-10 NIV)

Then God sent Elijah out to stand on the mountain, and He proceeded to send a terrible windstorm, followed by an earthquake, followed by a fire. The Lord was in none of these signs. Elijah observed all this, but in his depression he showed no reaction to these displays of power. Finally, Elijah heard a still, small voice. The Lord was present in that voice and Elijah hid his face. Finally, his focus began to change, and he saw God again. Yet, when the Lord asked him a second time, "What are you doing here, Elijah?" he feebly gave the same answer and excuses as before. However, after recognizing God, Elijah's answer likely sounded weak even to him this time. Elijah's depression and discouragement began to fade as he again turned his focus to God. What right did he have to be discouraged? The Almighty God, creator of heaven and earth, had also created Elijah. God had equipped him, and God had used him. He had used him in a mighty and marvelous way. If Elijah died now, he would go down in history for the things God had done through him, but if he lived, might God not use him again? What greater purpose could there be than to serve his Creator to whom he would also go when he left this world?

Yes, the Lord would use him again, for He was now verbally giving Elijah some commands. God gave him four clear instructions. First, "Go, return on your way to the wilderness of Damascus." Yes, he could do that. That was many days journey away, well over one-hundred miles, but he could do it. If only he had not fled to the desert, he would have been much closer, but he could and would retrace his steps. It would be great to be back doing work for the Lord. He would return from his wasted weeks to productivity for the Lord. He would return from self-pity to self-sacrifice.

Second, "When you arrive, anoint Hazael to be king over Syria." Anoint the king of Syria? Syria was Israel's enemy. Syria was a wicked, heathen nation. Was God even in control of who ruled in Syria? Might not Hazael kill Elijah? No, God had commanded and Elijah would obey. He could do this.

Third, "Anoint Jehu, son of Nimshi to be king over Israel." Yes, that would be a joy. The days of the wicked King Ahab and his evil wife Jezebel were numbered. Why had Elijah so feared Jezebel? How could he have forgotten that God was in control? Yes, he would love to anoint the new king of Israel. What a joy to serve the Lord!

Fourth, and finally, the Lord began, "Also...." By now Elijah was likely getting excited again. He was remembering the great joy of serving the Lord. You can imagine his mind crying, "Also what, Lord?" "Also," God continued, "anoint Elisha, son of Shephat from Abelmoholah to be prophet in your place." What? Had he heard right? No, not that! It has only been four years since he made his impact as God's prophet by foretelling the coming drought. He still had many good years left to serve God as His prophet to Israel. Isn't it too soon to anoint a replacement? Why is God telling him to do this now?

As he reflects on this final command and feels the pain that it brings, Elijah more clearly recognizes the foolishness of his recent discouragement. The work in which he had been involved was not Elijah's work, but God's work. The plan for Israel was not his plan, but God's plan. Yes, God could use Elijah in His plan, or He could use Elisha, or someone else. God did not need Elijah, but Elijah needed God. Elijah had been privileged to be used by God, but God uses men and women of faith, not men and women of discouragement. God uses those who focus on Him, not people who focus on themselves. What a great danger lies hidden in discouragement. It is the danger that you will miss out on an opportunity to be used by God. Elijah was now realizing that his discouragement was sin. He had forgotten the greatness of the God he served. He had forgotten that all of God's plans will be accomplished. Even if he was the only one left who served God, he should have rejoiced in the joy of service.

The Lord continues to tell Elijah the future. "Whoever escapes the sword of Hazael, Jehu will kill, and whoever escapes the sword of Jehu, Elisha will kill. However, I will spare seven thousand in Israel, none of whose knees have bowed to Baal and none of whose lips have kissed him." (I Kings 19:17-18 ML)

Yes, Elijah now fully understands. God's plans will be accomplished. Elijah's discouragement had been sin. Even his analysis of the situation had been wrong since he was far from the only one left who served God. He should never have been defeated because he and God were an unbeatable team. Surely he and God and the seven thousand others were destined for victory. If God would give him another chance, he would not allow discouragement to creep in and destroy his faith.

Despite his personal feelings, Elijah obeyed God. Without speaking to him, Elijah went and cast his mantel upon Elisha. He surely was not happy about passing on the mantel, but he obeyed. Elisha followed Elijah and became his servant from then on. God allowed Elijah eleven more years as His prophet before He took him home in a chariot of fire and the "propheting" work was left entirely to Elisha.

Elijah was unquestionably a great prophet of God. In Christ's day some even believed that Jesus was Elijah come back from the dead. He appeared with Moses and met Jesus on the Mount of Transfiguration. Some believe he will return again in the last days as one of the two witnesses spoken of in Revelation 11. However, he is not listed in Hebrews' Faith Hall of Fame. (Heb.11) Might that be because of his period of weak faith and discouragement?

You also need to beware of the danger of discouragement, for it is just as real today. In your athletic endeavors, things will happen that can easily cause you to become discouraged if your focus is wrong. When your faith cannot sustain you, when you are discouraged, you are not in a position to be used by God; you are not even able to please Him, for "Without faith it is impossible to please Him." (Hebrews 6:11a)

In 1997 Josh Cox was a fifth year senior at Liberty University and a distance runner. Because of a few bad choices as a freshman, he had gotten into some trouble and as a result had missed that outdoor season. Since then he had shown tremendous progress, both spiritually and athletically. He had exhausted his cross-country eligibility but still had one season of track eligibility left. Since he had no important competitions for the entire fall, he was running high weekly mileage to establish a good base for his final collegiate track season.

The chairman of the physical education department at Liberty, Dr. David Horton, is an unusual athlete. Although over fifty years of age, he is an extreme ultra-marathon runner. He held the record on the entire Appalachian Trail, which he ran from Georgia to Maine in less than fifty-three days. He also ran the third fastest time ever from California to New York. Obviously he is not your typical athlete.

Since Dr. Horton seems to have such a taste for unusual suffering, he has organized a race in the Appalachian Mountains, which he calls the 50-mile Mountain Masochist. The race is an October annual affair that has been conducted for over fifteen years. It draws some of the top ultra-marathon runners and trail runners in the country. The race is run over some very difficult terrain and involves elevation changes of nearly two miles vertically. The miles are what the runners call "Horton miles," which means that the race is probably closer to fifty-three miles. If you knew David Horton, you would understand this. Josh had done some long runs in the mountains with Dr. Horton and had helped him with race management in the past, so he was quite familiar with the race. As the fall began, Josh began to consider running that race, despite the fact that he had never before raced farther than 13.1 miles, a half marathon. Of course Dr. Horton fanned the flames of interest in Josh.

When Josh came to me as his head track coach to ask my opinion and permission to participate, I thought immediately that the idea was stupid at worse and unwise at best. The effort could set back his training a month or two, or worse yet, an injury could result that would have a greater negative effect. However, I remembered the badly sprained ankle that Josh had sustained just days before our conference championship a few years earlier, and I remembered how we had taken him to the cross country meet just to support his teammates. Then, suddenly feeling the compulsion to run, he had run the race in a fiberglass ankle brace and had helped our team to victory. I knew that day that the Lord had run through him, and perhaps again He wanted to do something that didn't make sense.

With many cautions, I gave my permission, praying that this would not prove to be a foolish decision. He also had plenty of advice from David Horton. However, one important piece of advice was never given. No one advised him to carry some anti-diarrheal medicine in his pouch.

The field of about two hundred runners left the starting line at 6:00 a.m. and Josh began running comfortably with the leaders. Despite his lack of experience, Josh believed he could win. The first three miles are on a flat road and the three leaders passed the three mile mark well under eighteen minutes. Things went well for Josh for nearly twenty miles but then he began to get the urge, as he says, to use the bushes. As he relieved himself, it was immediately apparent that his digestive system was not functioning properly. As quickly as possible, he was back on the trail and in a short time he caught back up to the leaders. He had not settled back into running very long when the urge came again. He tried to fight it off, but it was no use. Back he went into the bushes. The scenario repeated itself a few times and soon he could not catch back up to the leaders before he had to stop again. By thirty miles he had fallen back to fourth and the mileage, dehydration and discouragement were taking their toll.

The next ten miles were very difficult for Josh. His nearly one dozen trips to the bushes had also cost him valuable time. It was becoming clear that he was not going to achieve his goal. As he approached forty-three miles he was given the information that he was seven minutes behind Courtney Campbell, the leader who had set the course record the previous year. Of course Josh had been praying much of the race as he struggled against his body and his will. Now, however, he had reached the crucial point of decision. The compulsion to look at himself, to focus on his suffering, to bathe in his misery, was overwhelming. To allow himself to do that meant he would walk to the next aid station and catch a ride back to the finish line or reduce his effort but continue along and perhaps still manage a top ten finish.

However, as he came to the end of himself, he fully turned his eyes on God. Josh began to recite, out loud, a passage from Isaiah 40 that he had memorized years before. "Why do you say, O Jacob, and complain, O Israel, 'My way is hidden from the Lord, my cause is disregarded by my God?' Do you not know? Have you not heard? The Lord is the everlasting God, the Creator of the ends of the earth. He will not grow tired or weary, and His understanding no one can fathom. He gives strength to the weary and increases the power of the weak. Even youths grow tired and weary and young men stumble and fall; but they that wait upon the Lord shall renew their strength; they will mount up on wings like eagles; they shall run and not be weary; they shall walk and not faint."

As the words crossed his lips and entered his ears, Josh began to feel that strength that He gives to the weary. Some of the weakness seemed to evaporate from his legs and their power began to increase. The feeling of refreshment that entered his legs after nearly forty-five miles surprised him, but excited by it he recited the passage again, this time faster and louder. "Why do you say, O Joshua, and complain, O Josh...." He felt the power in his body continue to increase. "...gives strength...increase power...." His arms, instead of pumping, began to reach into the air toward God who was supplying the power. It was a very unusual sight, a young man running through the woods, arms stretched toward heaven, shouting a Scripture passage. He had become like Elijah running from Mount Carmel.

Afraid that the power might disappear, he continued to run faster and faster, repeating the passage time and time again. By the time he reached forty-seven miles, he had caught the leader. In the words of Courtney, "He flew by me at five minutes a mile." Josh rode that power all the way to the finish line, winning the race by nine minutes and thirty-six seconds, breaking the previous course record by two minutes and sixteen seconds.

Later that day Josh relived the excitement of feeling the power of God as he spoke to the other competitors and fans at the post-race supper. He gave the glory to God, because he knew that he had come to the end of himself out on that course, but when he looked to God, God proved Himself real. Christians who heard the testimony rejoiced, others shook their heads, but all marveled. The next week he shared the experience with 4000+ students and faculty in chapel at Liberty University and the Lord was honored. God used Josh that day because he avoided the danger of discouragement. His course record still stands at this writing as a testimony to the power of God in an exhausted runner who looked to Him. Josh accomplished his goal, but more importantly, Josh fulfilled God's plan for him on that fall day. The faith he gained that day spurred him on to bigger and better things. Two years later he became the youngest qualifier for the U.S. Olympic Trials in the marathon, and as we go to press in 2001, Josh has just finished as the U.S.A.'s top marathoner in the Track and Field World Championships.

Like Josh, every good athlete sets goals. As an athlete you should have a plan, an agenda, a list of goals that you want to accomplish. God also has a plan for you as an athlete. He has given you your athletic talents for a purpose. When your plan and His plan are in agreement, your plan will be accomplished. When your plan and His are different, and His plan, not yours, is fulfilled, you have no right to be discouraged. That is lack of faith. It is sin. As you learn to surrender your will to His will, you become a "surrendered Christian athlete," and you will learn to rejoice in the fulfillment of His plan. You will say with Paul, "And we **know** that all things work together for good to them that love God, to them who are the called according to His purpose." (Rom. 8:28 KJV) The surrendered Christian athlete will not be discouraged by failures, disappointments, or unfulfilled goals. He will dodge the danger of discouragement. He will always be available to be used by God.

Chapter 8
The Lessons of Failure

Success. Victory. Winner. Champion. These are words that bring a positive reaction to everyone, and especially to athletes. Failure. Defeat. Loser. Victim. Such words cause the exact opposite response. Despite the fact that these word groups are considered opposites, they can at times be very close together. Success or failure, victory or defeat, winning or losing can be the difference of a thousandth of a second. It can be the judgment of an official who makes an arbitrary decision on something that is in reality too close to call. It can depend on which way the football bounces or which way the wind happens to blow. Sometimes a single performance can be considered both of these opposites. When, in the 1976 Olympic Games, Shirley Babashoff won the Silver Medal in the 200m freestyle swimming event, but lost the gold by the world record performance of Kornelia Ender, a product of the East German drug-enhanced system, newspapers across the country proclaimed her as "loser, Shirley Babashoff." A similar disgrace was inflicted on Jim Ryan after his silver medal in the Mexico City 1500 meters. Both athletes had excellent performances but for reasons outside their control, someone else did better on that day. Both were labeled as losers by some writers who likely had no concept of all that was involved in their great performances. Were they losers, or were they winners?

The most basic definition of success is the achievement of a goal. Failure, by contrast, is falling short of a goal. If winning is the primary goal, anything but winning will be considered failure. If someone else's goal for you is higher than your own, you may consider yourself a success while he considers you a failure. Perhaps more often, an athlete's own goals are higher than others set for him, and while others consider him a success, he feels like a failure.

If you choose to only set goals that you are sure to achieve, you can avoid the feeling that you have failed, but such goals will not help you to reach your full potential. Reaching beyond your ability is the only way to find out how far you can really reach. In addition, there is a growth process, a learning experience, which takes place through failure. This growth helps the Christian athlete to surrender to God's will.

We have seen that God wants to bless His children, and that He is searching "back and forth across the whole earth, looking for people whose hearts are perfect toward Him, so that He can show His great power in helping them." Herein lies the first lesson of failure. Sometimes God allows His children to fail to help perfect their hearts toward Him. Failure may come as a punishment or as discipline from God.

"My son, do not make light of the Lord's discipline, and do not lose heart when He rebukes you, because the Lord disciplines those He loves, and He punishes everyone He accepts as a son. Endure hardship as discipline; God is treating you as son. For what son is not disciplined by his father?…God disciplines us for our good, that we may share in His holiness. No discipline seems pleasant at the time, but painful. Later on, however, it produces a harvest of righteousness and peace for those who have been trained by it." (Heb. 12:5-7, 10-11 NIV)

Failure and defeat help make people look inside themselves in a way that success and victory do not. Times of loss and disappointment are often times of self-examination and repentance. When you fail, you should first ask yourself, "Is there a reason that God is not blessing me? Is there unconfessed sin in my life? Is there a part of my life that I am not submitting to His Lordship? Is there a sinful attitude in my heart?" If you know what it is, confess it and turn from it. If you are not sure, ask the Lord to reveal it to you.

God's hand of blessing will not remain on a child of His who is living in sin. God may allow him some success for a time only to lift him up high enough that when he falls, he will be broken. A child of God can be sure that if he is living in sin, in God's perfect time, he will fall, for when discipline is required, God "disciplines those He loves."

"My son, despise not the chastening of the Lord; neither be weary of His correction: For whom the Lord loveth He correcteth: even as a father the son in whom he delighteth." (Prov. 3:11-12)

"Is God deaf and blind—He who makes ears and eyes? He punishes the nations—won't He also punish you? He knows everything —doesn't He also know what you are doing? The Lord is fully aware of how limited and futile the thoughts of mankind are, so He **helps us by punishing us.** This makes us follow His paths, and gives us respite from our enemies while God traps them and destroys them." (Ps. 94:9-13 TLB)

God's discipline is helpful in your growth process. His love demands that He mold you into the image of Christ. If your failure is discipline from God, confess and turn from your sin immediately. Do not have the experience of David, who said, "When I kept silent, my bones wasted away in my groaning all the day. For day and night Thy hand was heavy upon me; my marrow dried up as a summer drought." (Ps. 32:3-4 ML) Rather, confess as David finally did in Psalm 51 and have the "joy of your salvation" restored to you.

A second "lesson of failure" is a lesson which involves learning the character of God. Your failure may not be discipline from God to break or change you, but rather may be the polishing of God to make you shine more brightly. Paul wrote, "…we rejoice in our sufferings, knowing that suffering produces endurance, and endurance produces character…." (Rom. 5:3-4 RSV) As a mortal Christian, you sometimes follow the leading of the Holy Spirit and act in a situation as Christ would act. At other times, you get into your own humanity, in the flesh, and ignore or just don't hear the leading of the Spirit. Then you do not act as Christ would. As you grow in faith, God is working in your life to bring you to Christian maturity, to prepare you to act like Christ in an increasing number of situations. As you learn to endure setbacks, disappointments, and failures, the character of Christ is being formed in you. God at times allows such things for this very purpose.

A third lesson of failure involves learning the sufficiency of God's grace. Sometimes God may allow things to come into your life that you do not want, so that He can teach you what He taught Paul, that "My grace is sufficient for you, for my power is made perfect in weakness." (II Cor. 12:9 NIV) As you learn this lesson, you will gain a "peace that passes understanding." You will lose all fears, for you will be confident that whatever comes your way, God's grace will carry you through it.

Perhaps the verse most frequently quoted by athletes is Philippians 4:13, "I can do all things through Christ which strengtheneth me." Athletes often use this verse to try to stir themselves to greater performances, somehow implying that they can derive the strength to do anything from the spiritual source, Christ. A Christian athlete might say, "I know I can run a four-minute mile, because I can do all things through Christ who strengthens me." However, if he really can do "all things" through Christ, why is he aiming only for a four-minute mile? Why not a one-minute mile, or how about a five-second mile?

In reality, the context of Philippians 4:13 does not deal with our abilities as humans to accomplish feats through Christ's superhuman power, but with the knowledge of the sufficiency of God's grace. Paul wrote, "...I have learned, in whatever state I am, to be content. I know how to be abased, and I know how to abound; in any and all circumstances I have learned the secret of facing plenty and hunger, abundance and want." (Phil. 4:11-12 RSV) The Living Bible then states Philippians 4:13 this way: "for I can do everything God asks me to with the help of Christ who gives me strength and power." In the Modern Language translation we read, "I have strength for every situation through Him who empowers me." In other words, "God's grace is sufficient for me."

It would be good for you to fail miserably, over and over, in your athletic endeavors, until you know by experience the sufficiency of God's grace. When you learn this, you begin to experience the peace and joy God intends for His children. Then you will learn to say with Paul, "...in all these things we are more than conquerors through Him that loved us." (Rom. 8:37)

A fourth lesson of failure is not a lesson for you, but a lesson that others can learn through your failures. God may sometimes allow you to fail for the sake of someone else who is watching you. Often it is easier to show the character of God in defeat than in victory, in failure than in success. A Spirit-led Christian's manner of suffering is drastically different from the way a worldly person endures suffering, just as Christ's manner of suffering on the cross was drastically different from that of all other Roman crucifixions. "When the centurion and those who were with him keeping watch over Jesus saw what took place, they were filled with awe and said, "Truly this was the Son of God." (Matt 27:54 RSV) It has been said, "When you are squeezed, what is inside of you comes out." If Christ is within you, others may see Him in your suffering and they may be drawn to Him by your strength and hope in suffering.

Mary Decker Slaney was probably the greatest American female middle-distance runner in history. She entered the world scene as a high school sensation in the 1970s. She won several national titles, held several American records and medaled at the World Championships. However, somehow, an Olympic medal had eluded her. In 1984 she decided to focus on the 3000m at the Los Angeles Olympic Games to try to change that. She won her heat and easily advanced to the final. There she led most of the first half of the race. In the race was an eighteen-year old sensation, Zola Budd, who held Mary Decker as her hero. Just past 1700m Mary and Zola made contact and Mary suddenly fell down. That moment, which Mary saw as her worst moment, held the potential to be her greatest moment. The eyes of the world were upon her, waiting with great anticipation to see how she would respond to the sudden destruction of her dreams. Unfortunately she verbally lashed out at Zola and that is the picture of Mary that the world remembers. To expect her to respond as Christ would have responded is not realistic since she did not have the power of Christ within her. In such a moment even committed Christians often react in a way that dishonors the Lord. However, when a Christian in God's power responds like Jesus, the stark contrast to the response of the world is amazing and the testimony becomes very powerful. Sometimes God may allow you to experience failure and defeat to give you the opportunity to display this power to others.

A fifth lesson of failure is one that teaches you to trust God's timing. God scatters both minor and major victories and defeats throughout your life in such a way as to mold you and use you for His wonderful purpose. We are always striving for victories but it is the defeats that make the victories sweet. The more painful the defeats, the more exhilarating the victories.

From 1986 to 1994 Dan Jansen was arguably the greatest sprint speed skater in the world. He held the world record for 500m for most of that time. His first Olympics was the 1984 games where he gained valuable experience but didn't win a medal. By the 1988 Olympics in Calgary, Dan was the favorite for the gold medal in both the 500m and the 1000m. Just a few hours before the 500m his sister, Jane, died from leukemia. Skating the 500m, Dan Jansen fell, and the surest gold medal was gone. He had a second chance later in the week in the 1000m, and he was skating for his sister and her memory. As he headed down the straightaway, again he fell.

Four years later he was back at the Olympics Games representing the United States in Albertville. This time he just focused on the 500m. A slip in this short race caused him to finish 4th and the greatest sprint skater of all time was still without a medal after three Olympic Games.

A suggestion was made to the Olympic governing body that the Olympics would generate more interest if the winter Olympics were not held in the same year as the summer Olympics. A decision was made to stagger the events by two years, and, as a result, the next winter Olympics were held in 1994 in Lillehammer.

Dan set a new world record for 500m in 1993, so it was not a surprise to see him back at his fourth Olympic Games in 1994, but now a husband and father, he was likely at his final Olympics. He was again the favorite to win the 500m, but there was also much talk about his "Olympic jinx." Then, sure enough, though the fastest man on the ice, he slipped again and ended up without a medal. The US grieved with him, and the world grieved with him.

His final chance was the 1000m, but with his history and the pressure, the odds were strongly against him. Yet millions were drawn into his quest, and his final race became the focus of many people who generally had no interest in speed skating. His was a drama about to end. When the gun went off, he went out fast as many times before. At one point there was a slight slip, but he continued on without breaking form. As he came into the final homestretch it appeared that he might do it. With all his energy and skill he drove to the finish line, claiming the gold in a world record time, 1:12.43. The emotional response was incredible; the impact of the story immeasurable. The whole story was so much more powerful than it would have been if his Olympic history included several victories and medals. It seemed everyone wanted to know more about this man from Wisconsin.

Surely it would have been a lot easier for Dan Jansen to live out this drama if he had known all along how the story would end. Certainly the knowledge of the coming glory would have sustained him through the moments of heartbreak and disappointment, and those times of defeat would have been easier for him to bear. Do you realize that you, in fact, have the opportunity to do just that? As a surrendered Christian athlete, you are assured of an incredibly great coming glory. God is working and bringing you toward that day. He will bring it all about in His perfect timing. The story He is writing with your life is a great one indeed, but it's not over yet, so allow Him to write it and just keep turning the pages. Don't agonize over the things that don't turn out the way you want, but trust the great Author to create a work that will cause the reader to marvel, "being confident of this, that He who began a good work in you will carry it on to completion until the day of Christ Jesus."

Another lesson of failure is one that teaches you to gain an eternal perspective. This present, temporal life is short, "as a moment when it is past." Eternity is long, forever. Time compared to eternity is not even as a drop of water compared to all the world's oceans. When you begin to understand this perspective, God's perspective, you can learn to endure suffering with joy. As Paul said, "…we are the children of God, and if children, then heirs, heirs of God and fellow heirs with Christ, provided we suffer with Him in order that we may also be glorified with Him. I consider that the sufferings of this present time are not worth comparing with the glory that is to be revealed to us. (Rom. 8:16-18 RSV)

Jim Elliot, a missionary who was martyred for the gospel, once said, "He is no fool who gives what he cannot keep to gain what he cannot lose." Defeat, loss, suffering, and disappointment may at times result in greater rewards in the life to come. Knowing that, you can learn to "give thanks in all circumstances, for this is the will of God in Christ Jesus for you." (I Thess. 5:18 RSV)

Every earthly father who loves his children desires to bless his children and provide the best possible life for them. Even more so, your perfect, loving, heavenly Father desires to bless you, His child. When it appears that He is not blessing you, it may be a temporary condition to discipline you, to redirect you, or to teach you something that you need to learn. Or it may be an opportunity for you to point someone else toward Christ. Accept God's instruction with joy. Learn the lessons of failure quickly. Then you will be experiencing victory even in defeat.

Chapter 9
The Value of Victory

"Spanning the globe to bring you the constant variety of sport—the **thrill of victory** and the agony of defeat, the human drama of athletic competition." So for over a quarter of a century began the ever-popular ABC Wide World of Sports. It is unquestionably true that victory can be sweet, and when an athlete has tasted the "thrill of victory," he usually has a strong desire to feast at that table again. He naturally comes back trying to again satisfy that hunger. However, the thrill of victory is both fleeting and elusive.

The feeling is fleeting because the thrill and celebration only last a short time. The stands empty quickly, yesterday's paper becomes trash, the trophies collect dust, and the focus so soon turns back to training for the next competition.

The feeling is elusive because every victory makes it harder to experience the thrill of victory. Having achieved a measure of success, an athlete quickly sets a higher level of achievement as his goal. An athlete eliminated in the trials just wishes he "could have made the final." An athlete who made the final just wishes he "could have won a medal." The athlete who won the bronze would be happy if he just could have won silver. The silver medalist is disappointed because he almost won gold. And so on it goes.

Robert ran with the lead pack for the first mile of the five-mile cross-country race. On the second mile of the race his competitors dropped off the pace, one by one. By the time he passed the two-mile marker, Robert was alone. He went on to win the race by thirty seconds. After I congratulated him on his good race and his victory, he responded, "Thanks, but there was nobody in the race." Of course, he didn't really mean there was "nobody" in the race because obviously there were many other competitors. He meant that there was nobody so good that it was a thrill to defeat him. He had won, but the "thrill of victory" had eluded him. In reality, the thrill of victory is not a regular occurrence for athletes. In fact, the "agony of defeat" is a much more common experience. If the elusive thrill of victory is weighed against the frequent agony of defeat and the tremendous amount of work that is usually necessary to experience that thrill, one may well question whether or not the trouble is even worth it.

Nevertheless, many athletes are willing to pay an extreme price for that momentary thrill, for their "one moment in time." Whitney Houston sang a song by that name, a song that was very popular during the 1988 Olympics. The words of the song express this sentiment.

Each day I live, I want to be a day to give the best of me.
I'm only one, but not alone. My finest day is yet unknown.
I broke my heart for every gain. To taste the sweet,
I faced the pain. I rise and fall, yet through it all,
This much remains.
I want one moment in time,
When I'm more than I thought I could be.
When all of my dreams are a heartbeat away,
And the answers are all up to me.
Give me one moment in time,
When I'm racing with destiny.
Then in that one moment in time,
I will feel, I will feel eternity.
I've lived to be the very best. I want it all, no time for less.
I've laid my plans, now lay the chance here in my hands.
Give me one moment in time,
When I'm more than I thought I could be.
When all of my dreams are a heartbeat away,
And the answers are all up to me.
Give me one moment in time,
When I'm racing with destiny.

Then in that one moment in time,
I will feel, I will feel eternity.
You're a winner for a lifetime,
If you seize that one moment in time - Make it shine!
Give me one moment in time,
When I'm more than I thought I could be.
When all of my dreams are a heartbeat away,
And the answers are all up to me.
Give me one moment in time,
When I'm racing with destiny.
Then in that one moment of time,
I will be free.

It all sounds so good, but no moment will make you a winner for a lifetime, except that moment when you make Christ Lord of your life. The only important answer that is really all up to you is the answer to the question, "What will you do with Jesus?" A moment is a moment, and eternity is eternity. A moment means nothing compared to eternity, unless it affects eternity. One thrilling moment of success will not make you free, but "if the Son therefore shall make you free, ye shall be free indeed." (John 8:36 KJV) No, the thrill of victory is not the true value of victory.

One reason that the drive for even one moment of recognition and satisfaction is so great is because many people have low self-esteem and inadequate feelings of self worth. The desire for such a person to feel important even for a moment can be very powerful. When someone experiences success, when he accomplishes his goals, when he wins, his self image often improves and he gains confidence. Is this not a value of victory?

This may be true for an unsaved athlete, but it is not necessary for the truly surrendered Christian athlete. He recognizes that the Creator of the universe, the God of eternity, the controller of history, loves him so much that He gave His life for him. He knows the great value Christ has placed on his soul. He knows that even now Christ is preparing a place for him in heaven where he will spend eternity with Christ. He has no need for some athletic victory to help him feel that he has worth. He is already a child of the King.

Suppose, however, that you can reach a high enough level of success in athletics that you end up with fame and fortune. In today's world, many high level athletes are famous and are earning seven figure salaries. Athletic success can bring you celebrity status. Surely this must be a value of victory?

True, there is a blessing that goes along with popularity and wealth, but there can also be a curse. The task of becoming or remaining a surrendered Christian becomes more difficult. Jesus said, "I tell you the truth, it is hard for a rich man to enter the kingdom of heaven." (Matt. 19:23 NIV) It is hard to possess great fame and fortune and not become a slave to them. "No one can serve two masters. Either he will hate the one and love the other, or he will be devoted to the one and despise the other. You cannot serve both God and money." (Matt. 6:24 NIV)

Besides that, of what value is fame and fortune compared to that to which you are an heir as a child of God? "The Spirit Himself testifies with our spirit that we are God's children. Now if we are children, then we are heirs—heirs of God and co-heirs with Christ, if indeed we share in His sufferings in order that we may also share in His glory." (Rom. 8: 16-17 NIV) All the fame and fortune possible in this short lifetime appears insignificant when compared with the blessings and glory which we will share for all eternity because we are heirs with Christ. No, worldly fame and fortune are not the real value of victory.

However, there is value in victory, great value that should make you pursue victory with wholehearted dedication and enthusiasm. When victory is within reach, you should not be content to let it slip from your grasp. When you have not done your best and victory eludes you, you should determine to not allow that to happen again, because you may be missing the real value of victory.

We live in a world in which people take notice of victory and success. Everyone wants to win, and when people see a winner, they want to know about him and they want to be like him. The most successful athletes are the subjects of articles, are the focus of interviews, and are on the covers of magazines. People want to know how they feel, what they think, and what they do. Success can become a tremendous platform from which you can share your testimony of what Christ has done in your life. Your victory could help point someone toward Christ and that could make a difference that will count for eternity.

Reggie White, a 6' 5" three-hundred-pound lineman, holds the NFL career record for quarterback sacks. During his fourteen years in the National Football League he played in thirteen pro bowls, and in 1997 he led the Green Bay Packers to the Super Bowl championship. His athletic abilities have countless times placed him in a position where people would watch his actions and listen to his words. Throughout his athletic career he has taken a strong stand for the Lord.

Because of his athletic exploits, Reggie was given the opportunity to speak to the Wisconsin state legislature. He spoke openly about the problems facing our society and how they have resulted from our abandonment of Biblical principles. He spoke out against greed, immorality, including homosexuality, racial prejudice, and obscenity. His strong stance cost him a CBS football commentator contract and several other corporate sponsorships. However, Reggie White had already learned the real value of victory, which is far greater than million dollar contracts. His experience led him to write the book, *Fighting the Good Fight*, which daily continues to increase the value of his many victories.

Every Christian athlete, regardless of his skill level, has a platform that he should use to proclaim Christ. An unskilled or inexperienced athlete may have only a small sphere of influence through his athletics. Nevertheless, he should be faithful and diligent to reflect the light and love of Christ to that small group. He may have the opportunity to be a hero to just one young child, but the surrendered Christian athlete will avail himself of that opportunity.

Unfortunately, there is often a mindset among Christian athletes in which they think that if and when they reach some pinnacle of success, they will become an ambassador for the Lord. However, Christians always carry the name of Christ and are called to always be witnesses for Him. Young Christian athletes should learn to share Christ, "to always be prepared to give an answer to everyone who asks the reason for the hope that they have, with gentleness and respect." (I Peter 3:15) Then they will just need to continue to do what they have always done as the Lord gives greater successes and higher platforms from which to testify of God's goodness.

Your testimony could change the life and eternal destiny of a lost soul from this "depraved generation, in which you shine like stars in the universe as you hold out the word of life." (Phil. 2:15b-16a NIV) You have been chosen to reflect the light of Christ to the world. The brighter you shine, the more people there will be that can see the Light of the World in your life. There is also a great blessing in this for you, for "those who are wise will shine like the brightness of the heavens, and those who lead many to righteousness like the stars for ever and ever." (Daniel 12:3 NIV)

There is also a second related value of victory. Not only can your victories point someone to Christ, but they can also be a blessing to your Christian brothers and sisters. Your victories will illuminate your testimony, which may encourage them in their walk with the Lord. Your visible testimony may also challenge them to greater dedication and effort in their own calling from God. Your testimony may bring praise to their lips as you "let your light shine before men, that they may see your good deeds and praise your Father in heaven." (Matt. 5:16 NIV) As you experience greater victories, you will be able to strengthen more Christians with the testimony of God's work in your life.

Finally, there is a third value of victory that is exciting for a Christian to contemplate. It is possible for you, a mere mortal human, to bring glory to the name of Jesus Christ, the Lord of all creation, through your victories. Paul wrote, "…we pray constantly for you, that our God may count you worthy of His calling, and that by His power he may fulfill every good purpose of yours and every act prompted by your faith. We pray this so that the name of our Lord Jesus may be glorified in you, and you in Him, according to the grace of our God and our Lord Jesus Christ." (II Thess. 1:11-12 NIV) As you accomplish your own "good purpose" and complete the works that are "prompted by your faith," the name of the Lord Jesus is being glorified. You were created for this purpose, to have fellowship with God and to bring glory to Him. As Jesus said, "This is to my Father's glory, that you bear much fruit, showing yourselves to be my disciples." (John 15:8 NIV) What a joy it is to be able to honor your Creator in this way.

Therefore, pursue victory heartily in every athletic contest that you undertake. What other athlete has motivation as great as the surrendered Christian athlete? How can you be mediocre? What you accomplish may count for all eternity and may even now bring pleasure to Almighty God. Yes, indeed, there is great value in victory.

Chapter 10
The Armor of God

Carpus was a man of great physical prowess. He was a soldier by profession and well trained in the skill of combat. Strong, fit and agile, Carpus was an exemplary soldier and citizen in every way except for one. His crime was faith in Jesus Christ.

The year was A.D. 125. Many Christians had recently died in the Roman coliseums and today was to be his day. As he was led through the tunnel toward the open-air arena, he could hear the shouts of the crowd as another victim lost his life.

In a moment he was shoved through the gate to the floor of the coliseum. As his eyes adjusted to the sunlight, Carpus looked toward the center of the arena. There stood a muscular, well-armed gladiator. His weapons and armor were evidence that this was not intended to be a fair fight. The fight was expected to be a slaughter, satisfying the vicious appetite of the deranged spectators. Nevertheless, Carpus, knowing that the odds were against him, still believed that somehow he might win. He knew the importance of courage and a positive attitude from his years as a soldier and he was determined to give his best. Perhaps the crowd would admire his skill and courage and he would be spared.

The gladiator moved toward him with a spear in one hand and a flaming torch in the other. Carpus focused on the spear, which was soon flying straight at him. He dove left, narrowly eluding the spear, and after a quick roll he was back on his feet, focused on his nemesis again. The crowd roared. The warrior, now closer, pulled a dart from his leg sheath and lit it with his torch. Suddenly a streak of fire was coming even faster at Carpus. He dodged right and felt the breeze of the passing dart. Spectators screamed and applauded.

This might prove to be a better fight than most. The gladiator, clearly angered at his two failures, pulled three more darts from his quiver. He lit them and with one powerful throw sent all three hurling toward Carpus. Mustering all his athletic skill, Carpus managed to elude two of them, but the third stung his thigh. The crowd reacted as the searing pain of the puncture was compounded by the burning flame. Carpus grabbed the hot dart, burning his hand as he pulled it from his leg. His optimism began to fade.

A guard standing nearby was apparently impressed by Carpus' athletic ability, because he threw a shield to him. Carpus hobbled toward it and grabbed it for protection. With the shield he was able to parry a few more darts, but the gladiator threw down his torch and grabbed his spiked ball and chain and his sword from his belt. He drew near, wielding the sword in his left hand and swinging the spiked ball in his right. Carpus blocked a few blows from each, but then the ball bounced off the shield and hit him on the side of the head. Things went black and as the crowd shouted its approval, the gladiator killed Carpus.

A real life drama similar to this fictitious story may have occurred during the early century persecutions of Christians. However, this story is intended as an analogy of the battle that so many Christians are fighting today. Christians are in a war. "…we are not fighting against people made of flesh and blood, but against persons without bodies—the evil rulers of the unseen world, those mighty satanic beings and great evil princes of darkness who rule this world: and against huge numbers of wicked spirits in the spirit world." (Eph. 6:12 TLB)

When a non-Christian goes into this battle, he has less chance of surviving than Carpus had. He has no offense and no defense and he will fail. But sadly, often Christians also go into the battle ill equipped. When a person accepts Christ as his Savior, he becomes a member of the faith. He receives his shield of faith. This shield of faith is a crucial part of the armor of God, but it is not all that is necessary to win the battle. Even as the skilled Carpus was not prepared to win with just a shield, neither are Christians today. Therefore, Paul exhorts us to "put on the full armor of God, so that you can take your stand against the devil's schemes." (Eph. 6:11 NIV) And again, "Therefore, put on the full armor of God, so that when the day of evil comes, you may be able to stand your ground, and after you have done everything, to stand." (Eph. 6:13 NIV)

You are Carpus. The gladiator is Satan or any number of his wicked spirits. If you intend to win your spiritual battles, you'd better listen to the coach who tells you how to equip yourself to win. Hear His instructions from Ephesians 6. "Put on the belt of truth." This is your identification with Jesus Christ. Jesus said, "I am the way, the **truth**, and the life." Jesus Christ also said, "I came into the world to testify to the truth. Everyone on the side of truth listens to me." (John 18:37b NIV) You need to start by taking your stand with Christ.

"Have the breastplate of righteousness attached firmly in place." The breastplate of righteousness must be properly placed to guard your heart. God desires to fill your heart with His love. Satan desires to harden your heart against God. One of his best ways to destroy you is by getting to your heart. As Jesus said, "What comes out of a man is what makes him unclean. For from within, out of men's hearts, come evil thoughts, sexual immorality, theft, murder, adultery, greed, malice, deceit, lewdness, envy, slander, arrogance and folly." (Mark 7:20-22 NIV) These things have no place with righteousness, and the breastplate of righteousness will protect your heart from them and their destructive effects.

"On your feet put the proper shoes, shoes that will help speed you to proclaim the gospel of peace." Athletes know how important it is to wear the proper shoes when participating in an athletic event. Imagine trying to play football in bowling shoes. And don't wear your track spikes to the bowling alley. Even as we engage in spiritual battles, we must not forget our orders to proclaim the good news of peace, the peace that you have in your heart and God's promise of peace on earth. Through Christ you have peace with God, and the good news is that this is available to everyone who will open his heart to Him. We are called to aggressively pursue this mission.

"Take up the shield of faith, which can quench all the flaming darts of the evil one." Satan and his forces are experts in the many different forms of evil. He has an arsenal of fiery darts with which he will try to destroy you. He quickly discovers which types work best on you, and he will especially use those. He has darts of dishonesty and deceit, darts of sexual impurity and lust, darts of materialism and covetousness, darts of selfishness and pride, darts of envy and hatred, darts of disobedience and rebellion, darts of gossip and corrupt speech, darts of dissatisfaction and complaint, darts of anger and malice, and many variations of these weapons.

However, you can protect yourself from these attacks using the shield of faith. If your faith is small, your protection will be limited. If your faith is large, your protection will be great. Your life should be focused on increasing your faith, on learning to trust God and His Word more and more and acting upon that trust. Even as your body gets stronger as you do regular physical exercise, so your faith will be made stronger by regular spiritual exercise. You should repeatedly put your faith to the test by attempting tasks that require stronger faith. By this exercise, your faith will grow. As you do this, the powers of darkness will encounter greater difficulty in their efforts to injure you.

"Put on the helmet of salvation." This helmet will protect your mind, which along with the heart are the main targets of Satan's offense. When salvation is on your mind, Satan will not be able to set your mind on earthly things. "For those who live according to the flesh set their minds on the things of the flesh, but those who live according to the Spirit set their minds on the things of the Spirit. To set the mind on the flesh is death, but to set the mind on the Spirit is life and peace. For the mind that is set on the flesh is hostile to God; it does not submit to God's law, indeed it cannot;

and those who are of the flesh cannot please God." (Rom. 8:5-9 RSV)

All this armor that is available to you is protective and for defense, but you cannot win a battle with only defense. So finally, "take up the sword of the Spirit, which is the Word of God." This is your weapon of attack. This is that which will allow you to defeat the enemy and to send him running away injured. Your sword makes it possible for you to have victory in the spiritual battle, but you have to know how to use it.

When the forces of evil attack you, you cannot just grab the Bible and swing it at them. That will not scare or hurt them. You have to know what the Bible says in order to counter the attacks. They want you to sin and suffer sin's consequences. David wrote, "Thy Word have I hid in my heart, that I might not sin against thee." (Ps. 119:11 KJV) Jesus, when tempted by Satan in the wilderness, each time answered Satan, "It is written," and then quoted the Scripture that exposed the evil in the action that Satan was suggesting. If even Christ, who has all authority in heaven and on earth, used the Word of God to combat the devil, how much more should we?

A Christian's life should be one of "growing in grace and the knowledge of the Lord." This can only be done through study of the Holy Scriptures. To be a successful athlete, you obviously have to train. To gain victory in your spiritual battles, you must also train, train to know and use the Bible. You must read it, study it, memorize it, and meditate on it. Then you will become more skilled at spiritual warfare and it will be more difficult for those "evil rulers of the unseen world" to win a victory over you. Certainly this is not easy. The Bible is a thick book, with much difficult reading. Yet, with increased reading and study, a Christian gains an increased love for the Book, for it imparts heavenly wisdom to him. If you fail to spend time in God's Word, do not expect to win your battles against the principalities and rulers of this present darkness. However, if you put on the whole armor of God and faithfully and systematically take up the sword of the Spirit, you can expect to win victories that will be greater and more important than those you may win on the athletic field. You can defeat the powers of darkness and the prince of this world. You can become a great spiritual athlete. What better victories can you win?

Chapter 11
The Attitude for Altitude

"A man's courage can sustain his broken body, but when courage dies, what hope is left?" (Prov.18:14 TLB) This statement is true in battle, whether that battle is taking place on a battleground or on an athletic field. Hope of victory and the courage to persist will enable an athlete to continue to make an extreme effort, but when the prospect seems hopeless, the athlete's energy quickly fades. The home stretch of a race of any distance is a very different experience to the athlete depending upon whether or not he is accomplishing his goal. In both cases his body is fatigued and his energy is spent, but hope of imminent victory appears to energize him whereas the prospect of inevitable defeat weakens him.

This is true of teams as well as of individuals and it is the basis of the concept of "momentum" in athletics. When a team has fought its way back from a major deficit, the players begin to believe that they will go on to victory even though they may still be losing. The team that is winning has seen its lead quickly disappear and the players begin to sense that they may lose the game. The team that is losing appears ready to win while the team that is winning seems ready for defeat. The attitude of an entire team can easily be greatly affected by these circumstances. "Momentum" can be more important than the score at the moment.

Certainly there is no question that an athlete's attitude has a profound effect upon what he can accomplish, that his "attitude" affects his "altitude." The well-known preacher, Charles Swindoll, has said about attitude,

> Words can never adequately convey the incredible impact of our attitude toward life. The longer I live, the more

convinced I become that life is 10 percent what happens to us and 90 percent how we respond to it. I believe the single most significant decision I can make on a day to day basis is my choice of attitude. It is more important than my past, my education, my bankroll, my successes or failures, fame or pain, what other people think of me or say about me, my circumstances, or my position. Attitude keeps me going or cripples my progress. It alone fuels my fire or assaults my hope. When my attitudes are right, there's no barrier too high, no valley too deep, no dream too extreme, and no challenge too great for me.

Notice that Swindoll correctly identifies attitude as a choice. We either consciously or subconsciously choose the attitude that we bring to every situation. Though we usually feel that our attitudes are the results of our circumstances, more often our circumstances are the results of our attitudes.

Since attitude so greatly affects outcome, we will do well to focus our attention upon the attitude of the surrendered Christian athlete. What should his attitude be as he faces athletics and as he faces life? What attitude does he adopt to bring honor to Jesus Christ?

It is not necessary for us to piece together lessons and examples from the Scriptures to answer this question. Paul answers this question directly in the second chapter of Philippians.

"Your attitude should be the same as that of Christ Jesus: Who being in very nature God, did not consider equality with God something to be grasped, but made Himself nothing, taking the very nature of a servant, being made in human likeness. And being found in appearance as a man, He humbled Himself and became obedient to death—even death on a cross! Therefore God exalted Him to the highest place and gave Him the name that is above every name, that at the name Jesus every knee should bow, in heaven and on earth and under the earth, and every tongue confess that Jesus Christ is Lord, to the glory of God the Father." (Phil. 2: 5-11 NIV)

This passage brings out one of the great paradoxes of the Christian life. It is an example of how even "the foolishness of God is wiser than men." (I Cor. 1:25a) Paul is telling us that the way to go up is to go down. The way to gain altitude is to lose altitude. To be exalted, you must humble yourself, for "he that humbleth himself shall be exalted." (Luke 14:11b KJV)

Have you ever seen an eagle or a hawk soar hundreds or even thousands of feet above the ground? Such birds are rarely seen flapping their wings, yet they are so much higher than the altitude at which most birds fly, despite all the wing flapping that other birds do. These high fliers reach such altitudes by riding on the thermals, that is, the rising currents of hot air. They hold a strong, steady wing position and allow the rising air to lift them up. They could not attain such great altitude on their own strength, but they find the right source of power to rise to great heights. That power cannot be seen, but it is there and is available to them.

There is no way for you, in your own power, to reach the heights to which God can lift you. If you develop the attitude of Christ, the Bible promises that God will elevate you. "If you will humble yourselves under the mighty hand of God, in His good time He will lift you up." (I Peter 5:6 TLB) Believe this promise and trust Him for the timing.

So often we think that it is by our own hard work that we will reach great heights. We flap our wings to the point of fatigue and then we cannot hold the strong position we need to ride the thermals. Rather, we should be strong and confident in the power of God, "strong in the Lord, and the power of His might." (Eph. 6:10 KJV) This is not to say that we shouldn't work hard to achieve our goals, but our hard work, our very best efforts, should be, as we saw in Chapter 4, our sacrifice to God. We should allow Him to determine when we will reach our greatest height and how high that altitude will be.

Christ's attitude was not merely one of humility but also one of obedience. He was "obedient unto death, even the death of the cross." (Phil. 2:8 KJV) He submitted His will to the will of the Father.

Once when his disciples were trying to encourage Jesus to eat, He replied, "I have food to eat that you know nothing about…. My food is to do the will of Him who sent me and to finish His work." (John 4:32, 34 NIV) Jesus never complained about the Father's will for Him. Even when that will was in opposition to His own "human" will, He did not complain. In the garden, just before the crucifixion that He knew was coming, He prayed, "Father, if you are willing, take this cup from Me; yet not My will, but Yours be done." (Luke 22:42 NIV)

Such an attitude is rarely seen today. Even Christians can frequently be heard complaining about circumstances or situations. It is so easy to "get in the flesh" when plans we have made are foiled and things don't go our way. It often appears that whatever high altitude we attain, we always want more. It is so much easier for us to focus on disappointments than to count blessings. Yet, if the circumstances that unfold in our lives are according to God's will, why should we complain? How dare we complain? We need to learn to say with Paul, "Therefore I will boast all the more gladly about my weaknesses, so that Christ's power may rest on me. That is why, for Christ's sake, I delight in weaknesses, in insults, in hardships, in persecutions, in difficulties. For when I am weak, then I am strong." (II Cor. 12:9b-10 NIV)

God sees the entire picture. He knows His plan. He knows your past, present and future. He knows your heart and He knows your needs far better than you know them yourself. Learn to put your life in His hands and be assured that "in all things God works for the good of those who love Him, who have been called according to His purpose." (Romans 8:28 NIV) Allow Him to take you to the height that He has planned. Be a surrendered Christian athlete and develop the attitude for altitude.

Chapter 12
The Will of God: The Word of God

"It must be God's will." These are words that I frequently hear since I work primarily with Christian athletes and live in a largely Christian community. Often I hear these words spoken when things have not turned out according to the plans of the person speaking the words and he uses this idea to help him accept his disappointment. I have at times referred to this phrase as "the Christian cop-out" because I have seen many cases in which it appears to me that an unfulfilled goal is really the result of inadequate preparation or undisciplined focus rather than "God's ordained will." However, we have already seen that there are lessons in failure, and there certainly may be times when a disappointment or loss may be "God's will."

Among Christian young people there appears to be considerable interest in "the will of God." Many of what seem to be life's major decisions—"What career shall I pursue? Whom should I marry? Where should I live? Which job offer should I accept?"—come during the early adult years. These decisions naturally lead a Christian young man or woman to wonder about what God's will is in these situations. You may be pondering a decision right now about which you wish God would reveal His will. Choosing a path, when you don't know what lies down that path, can be an intimidating experience. The fear of making a "wrong" decision creates the desire to pass that decision on to God. In that way no major decision would prove to be a mistake.

However, there is a major difference between wanting God to make a decision or two for you, and desiring to know God's will. In the case of the former, you may try familiar tactics such as praying, consulting a pastor or spiritual leader, randomly opening a Bible and reading a passage, or "putting out a fleece." (Judges 6) Although none of these actions are wrong in themselves, these are not the way to accomplish the latter. The best way to get to know God's will is to get to know God.

There have probably been times in your life when you knew your mother's will about something even though she had never expressly explained how she felt about that particular thing. Yet, because you knew her and knew her well, you knew how she would feel about it. Similarly, when we get to know God, we will know His will in many important situations.

God has revealed some things about Himself in nature. As Paul wrote, "For since the creation of the world God's invisible qualities—His eternal power and divine nature—have been clearly seen, being understood from what has been made, so that men are without excuse." (Romans 1:20 NIV)

God has revealed Himself much more completely in His Holy Word. To get to know God intimately, we must go to His Word. The person of God and the will of God are found in the Bible. It is surprising how often we Christians claim to be seeking God's will and yet we spend little time reading, studying, memorizing and meditating on God's Word.

It is logical that God would reveal Himself and His will in written form. When God first spoke to the Israelites from Mount Sinai, the people said to Moses, "Speak thou with us, and we will hear: but let not God speak with us, lest we die." (Ex. 20:19 KJV) God later told Moses, "Thou canst not see my face: for there shall no man see me, and live." (Ex. 33:20 KJV) Therefore God cannot reveal Himself to us face to face.

The most basic means of communication, other than face to face, is the written word. It is a sure means of communicating a constant and true message. That God has chosen to reveal Himself through a written book is no surprise. The Bible is the most enduring book of all time and it continues as the most printed, most sold and most read book in history. Many laud the Bible as the greatest book in history, but too few are willing to work at applying its instructions to their lives.

We call God's written Word the Holy Bible. If it is truly God's Word, it is of necessity holy and without error, because God by nature is perfect and incapable of any error. Questions about authenticity arise primarily because God used ordinary men to write the Bible and man in himself is incapable of writing a holy book. However, God the Holy Spirit inspired each of the many authors as he wrote God's Word. The entire scriptures were written in this manner for "All Scripture is given by inspiration of God, and is profitable for doctrine, for reproof, for correction, for instruction in righteousness: That the man of God may be perfect, thoroughly furnished unto all good works." (II Tim. 3:16-17 KJV)

Not only were the Scriptures "God-breathed," that is, written under the inspiration of the Holy Spirit, but they can also be interpreted and understood by the reader with the guidance of that same Holy Spirit. This phenomenon is referred to as the "illumination of the Spirit." As Jesus predicted, "...the Counselor, the Holy Spirit, whom the Father will send in my name, He will teach you all things...." (John 14:26 RSV) Again in the words of Paul, "... the anointing which you received from Him abides in you, and you have no need that any one should teach you; as His anointing teaches you about everything, and is true, and is no lie, just as it has taught you, abide in Him." (I John 2:27 RSV)

In the words of Billy Graham, "The Holy Spirit illumines the minds and open the hearts of its [the Bible's] readers.... The reading of Scripture itself enables the Holy Spirit to enlighten us and do His work in us. While we read the Word, its message saturates our hearts, whether we are conscious of what is happening or not. The Word with all its mysterious power touches our lives and gives us its power.... This has been my experience as I have studied the Scriptures. Things I have known intellectually for years have come alive to me in their fuller spiritual significance almost miraculously. As I have studied the Scriptures, I have also learned that the Spirit always lets more light shine from the Word. Almost every time I read an old, familiar passage I see something new. This happens because the written Word of God is a living Word. I always come to the Scriptures with the Psalmist's prayer, 'Open my eyes, that I may behold wonderful things from Thy law'" (Ps. 119:18). Billy Graham - *The Holy Spirit* (pgs. 65-67)

As you read and study the Word of God, go to it with the expectation that He will speak to you. Pray that the Spirit will illuminate the "Word of God" to you. Much of what you hear will be applicable for all men, but often you will hear a message that applies specifically to you at your point of need. God will lead, guide and direct you in your life by your careful study of His Word. There may even be times when He will say something to you by a passage that no one else would hear. Allow me to relate one such experience in my own life.

In 1991, Liberty University track, for which I serve as head coach, joined the Intercollegiate Amateur Athletic Association of America, the oldest and largest collegiate conference in the United States. This conference, known as the IC4A, holds memberships of over one-hundred universities and colleges, mostly from the Northeast, but including colleges as far west as Notre Dame and as far south as Duke. When we joined that organization, we knew that our team had a long way to go in order to become competitive at that level. I was certainly pleased when we placed 24th in our first IC4A outdoor championship.

The following two years our team placed 14th and 11th before surprising many, including ourselves, with a 2nd place finish in 1994. After such a dramatic climb, we set our goal to win in 1995. George Mason University had won the previous six championships, most of them by a considerable margin, so our goal was certainly ambitious. When a series of setbacks and injuries sent us to the meet with only half of our expected participants, it was apparent that our goal was unrealistic. However, even with such a small representation, several amazing things happened that allowed the Liberty team to again place second, although only 3 1/2 points ahead of Georgetown University, which finished five places back in 7th. Sandwiched in between were Pittsburgh, West Virginia, Princeton, and Seton Hall. George Mason's international squad again ran away with the meet, winning by a margin of over two to one.

It seemed clearly apparent to me that the 2nd place finish was a gift from God, and I began to believe and pray that we could win the next year. Several of our athletes that had seen what happened in 1995 also began to believe. We set the 1996 IC4A victory as our season's goal.

As we approached 1996, our pastor and school chancellor, Jerry Falwell, began to challenge many people to read through the entire Bible in the coming year. I accepted the challenge and also invited our coaches and athletes to join me in the venture. I was pleasantly surprised when the entire team agreed to join in the undertaking. For the new year we had an ambitious spiritual goal and a monumental athletic goal.

Unfortunately, at least to most of our fans, George Mason had an extremely strong team in 1996. In early March they dethroned Arkansas as the NCAA indoor national champion, ending Arkansas' string of twelve straight NCAA indoor national championships. Our goal then looked impossible. *Track and Field News* wrote in their conference championship preview, "George Mason is strongly favored to write even deeper in the 120-year history book of America's oldest collegiate meet and run its consecutive-titles record to eight."

Yet, for some reason, I continued to believe that we could win. Through parents and supporters we amassed a significant group of people who were praying to that end. I personally fasted and prayed, asking God for victory.

On the day that we left for the meet, my wife asked me, "With all this talk about winning the IC4A championship, what really is the chance?" I hesitated a moment and then answered, "Without divine intervention? Zero percent. With divine intervention? One-hundred percent."

The first three days of the four-day meet went quite well for our team and surprisingly not very well for George Mason's team. Several of their high-level field event athletes performed poorly. As we went to the hotel at the end of the third day, it actually appeared that there was a realistic possibility that we could win.

The next morning my annual Bible reading guide had me reading in I Chronicles 4, reading the genealogies of the clans of Judah. I was seeking a word from the Lord, but instead I was reading names that I could barely pronounce. "Naarah bore him Ahuzzam, Hepher, Temeni and Haahashtari. These were the descendants of Naarah. The sons of Helah: Zereth, Zohar, Ethnan, and Koz, who was the father of Anub and Hazzobebah and of the clans of Aharhel, son of Harum." (I Chr. 4:6-8 NIV) I was thinking, "What am I supposed to get out of this?" Nevertheless, I continued, "Jabez was more honorable than his brothers. His mother had named him Jabez, saying, 'I gave birth to him in pain.' Jabez cried out to the God of Israel, 'Oh, that you would bless me and enlarge my territory! Let your hand be with me, and keep me from harm so that I will be free from pain.' And God granted his request." (I Chr. 4:9-10 NIV)

"And God granted his request!" The words jumped off the page at me. It was as if I'd heard the Spirit shout them in my ear. Jabez had asked and God had answered. I had asked and I sensed that He was answering. Words I had probably read before that previously had no meaning to me suddenly became alive. Certainly no Bible scholar would agree that these words meant that we would win that day. However, I finished my devotions sensing that God had spoken to me personally through these five words from His Word, spoken in a way that uniquely met my need of the day. I went into the day eager to see what God would do.

The next morning the *Sport News* reported, "A funny thing happened on the way to George Mason's eighth consecutive IC4A title…Liberty University, a school backed by the power of God, had the sun shine on them. Liberty had what could only be described as a performance of Biblical proportions." The request had been granted: Liberty - 93, GMU - 88.

God's Word is alive and the Holy Spirit will speak to you through it as you faithfully read and study it. Occasionally He may shout to you, but usually He will speak in His still, small voice. If you will quiet your heart, you will hear. You will come to know the will of God. You will come to love the Word of God.

Chapter 13
The Will of God: The Voice of the Spirit

W e have seen that God's Word communicates His will and that an increased knowledge and understanding of His Word produces an increased knowledge and understanding of His will. There is, however, a second means by which God communicates to man. Often He will communicate His will in this way.

I approach this subject with extreme caution, knowing that this topic might better be addressed by a theologian or Bible scholar than by a coach, but then, when is the last time that an athlete like you read a book written by a theologian? Therefore, with much care, I will proceed.

The second means by which God communicates to His people is by the "Voice of the Spirit." Having on occasion clearly "heard" this voice and learned from it, I believe that it is important for you to be alert for this phenomenon in your own Christian walk. The surrendered Christian athlete learns to listen for this voice. Christ said in John 10:4, "And when he [the shepherd] brings out his own sheep, he goes before them; and the sheep follow him, for they know his voice." Again in John 10:27 he said, "My sheep hear my voice, and I know them, and they follow me." Recognizing His voice can help you follow Him. Finally, John 8:47 says, "He who belongs to God hears what God says."

God exists in every Christian in the person of the Holy Spirit. The entrance of God the Holy Spirit into a person takes place at the time that an individual accepts Christ as His Savior. This occurrence is sometimes referred to as being "born again." Christ told Nicodemus, "Except a man be born again, he cannot see the kingdom of God." (John 3:3 KJV) "Verily, verily, I say unto you, except a man be born of water and of the Spirit, he cannot enter into the kingdom of God. That which is born of flesh is flesh: and that which is born of the Spirit is spirit." (John 3:5-6 KJV) Being "born of water" or "of flesh" is physical birth. Every living human has been born from his mother with the breaking of her water, born as flesh into the world. Not every human has experienced the second birth, being born of the Spirit, but all who have experienced it have the Holy Spirit living in their bodies.

Paul wrote to Christians, "Do you not know that you are God's temple and that the Spirit of God dwells in you?" (I Cor. 3:16 ML) Later he wrote, "What agreement has God's temple with idols? For we are the temple of the living God, as God has said, 'I will dwell in them, and walk among them, and I will be their God and they shall be My people.'" (II Cor. 6:16 ML)

The Holy Spirit is probably the least understood person of the Holy Trinity. Though as God He is unchanging, His work has changed through the various periods of history. He was involved in creation, for we read in Genesis 1:2 that "the Spirit of God moved upon the face of the waters." During Old Testament times the Spirit "came upon" men, and He accomplished things through these men that were according to His will. For example, He "came upon" Samson, for we read, "Then the Spirit of the Lord came upon him and he tore him [the lion] apart as one might tear apart a kid of the goats, although he had nothing in his hand." (Judges 14:6 ML) Yet, even as He "came upon" men, he also departed from them. We read later that after Delilah cut Samson's hair "he awoke out of his sleep and said, 'I will go out as at other times and shake myself free.' He did not know that the Lord had departed from him." (Judges 16:20 ML)

Since Pentecost the Holy Spirit has had a different work to do. Christ told His disciples, "Nevertheless I tell you the truth: it is to your advantage that I go away, for if I do not go away, the Counselor [Holy Spirit] will not come to you; but if I go, I will send Him to you." (John 16: 7 RSV) On the day of Pentecost, when all of the disciples of Christ were filled with the Holy Spirit, Peter explained to those who had gathered to see what was happening, "…we are all witnesses that Jesus rose from the dead. And now He sits on the throne of highest honor in heaven, next to God. And just as promised, the Father gave Him the authority to send the Holy Spirit— with the results you are seeing and hearing today." (Acts 2:32b-33 TLB) This spiritual rebirth happened not only to Christ's disciples, but it has also been a real experience for every Christian since then. Paul wrote, "You are not in the flesh, you are in the Spirit, if in fact the Spirit of God dwells in you. Any one who does not have the Spirit of Christ does not belong to Him." (Romans 8:9 RSV) In other words, if you do not have the Spirit of God, [the Spirit of Christ, the Holy Spirit] within you, you are not a Christian. You are not born again. In your present state you "cannot see the kingdom of God."

The Counselor, or Holy Spirit, speaks, gives advice, and even at times gives a glimpse of the future. Christ explained, "But when He, the Spirit of truth, comes, He will guide you into all truth. He will not speak on His own; He will speak only what He hears, and He will tell you what is yet to come. He will bring glory to me by taking from what is mine and making it known to you. All that belongs to the Father is mine. That is why I said the Spirit will take from what is mine and make it known to you." (John 16:13-15 NIV) The reference to the Spirit speaking does not mean that He speaks in an audible voice that we hear with our physical ears. Rather, "The Spirit itself beareth witness with our spirit…." (Romans 8:16 KJV)

Every man is created in the image of God, as a trinity: spirit, mind and body. While that man is alive his spirit lives in his body. When he dies his spirit departs from his body. We know this from the Word of God, but many people who have had near-death experiences have also recalled experiences involving their spirits leaving their bodies. When a man accepts Christ, as we have just seen from the Scripture, the Holy Spirit comes to live with his own spirit in his body. Is it any wonder that two spirits living in the same body would communicate? Although the ears on the side of your head may not be able to hear the voice of the Spirit, your spirit can hear His voice. You can come to know things in your spirit.

If you are a Christian, you have certainly experienced this. You have sensed the Spirit convicting you of your sin and your need for a savior. You have sensed the Spirit striving with your spirit as you considered the claims of Christ on your life. In Genesis 6:3, God said, "My Spirit shall not strive with man forever." The Holy Spirit strives with the spirit of man trying to convince him of the truth of the gospel message and attempting to get him to accept the salvation offered through Jesus Christ. You could not have been saved without hearing the "voice of the Spirit." You are saved because you responded to the call and conviction of the Spirit.

You also have assurance of your salvation by the "voice of the Spirit" for "the Spirit also beareth witness with our spirits that we are the children of God." (Romans 8:16) This communication between the Spirit of God and the spirit of man is a reality even though it may be difficult to understand. God can communicate a message to you that you will know even though you never read it or physically heard it. For lack of a better way to describe this, people who have experienced this may say that they "sensed" it. Have you ever attended a particularly moving service where you "sensed" the presence of the Lord? You did not see Him or hear Him, but you knew He was there. You knew "in your spirit."

At this point I feel it is necessary to raise a bright caution flag. You can easily get excited about the thought of God communicating directly with you and it is appealing to think about living each day with God constantly telling you what to do. However, many terrible things have been done by people who claimed that they were "doing what God told them to do." Usually cult leaders claim to have received a supernatural message from God in which He told them to lead their followers as they are leading. They may just be saying that to try to get a following or they may actually have received a spiritual message. The fact is that the Holy Spirit is not the only spirit capable of communicating with your spirit. Evil spirits can also communicate with your spirit. Therefore, when you "sense" something in your spirit, it is possible that the message is from the Prince of Glory or from the prince of darkness. You need to know the source of the spiritual message before you act on it.

The apostle John wrote, "Dear Friends, do not believe every spirit, but test the spirits to see whether they are from God.... This is how you can recognize the Spirit of God: Every spirit that acknowledges that Jesus Christ has come in the flesh is from God, but every spirit that does not acknowledge Jesus is not from God." (I John 4:1-3 NIV) The first test of a spirit is the Jesus Christ test. Evil spirits desire to defame the name of Christ. The Holy Spirit desires to glorify the name of Christ. Is the spiritual message you think you are receiving one that will defame or glorify Christ? Will it advance or hinder the cause of Christ?

The second test is the Bible test. Is the message you are sensing in conformity with the Word of God? The Spirit cannot contradict Himself. The Word He inspired in the Scriptures and any other word He gives must be in unity. If a man claims that the Spirit is telling him to leave his wife for another woman, we can be sure the spirit he is hearing from is not of God because the Bible says, "What therefore God has joined together, let not man put asunder." (Matt. 19: 6 RSV) No message received from the "voice of the Spirit" can contradict Scripture.

As you live the surrendered Christian life and grow in your relationship with Christ, you will improve your ability to recognize the Spirit's voice. Paul wrote, "Do not conform any longer to the pattern of this world, but be transformed by the renewing of your mind. Then you will be able to test and approve what God's will is—His good, pleasing, and perfect will." (Rom. 12:2 NIV) This renewing of your mind takes place daily as you study the Word of God and walk in the Spirit. "Though our outer nature is wasting away, our inner nature is being renewed every day." (II Cor. 4:16 -RSV) The Holy Spirit is the one orchestrating this renewal, for God "saved us through the washing of rebirth and renewal by the Holy Spirit." (Titus 3:5 NIV)

Because of the danger involved in discerning spiritual messages, many Christians avoid listening for the Spirit's voice. This is not the wise pathway to choose. Paul warned the church at Thessalonica, "Do not put out the Spirit's fire; do not treat prophecies with contempt. Test everything. Hold on to the good. Avoid every kind of evil." (I Thess. 5:19-22 NIV)

The Holy Spirit can communicate a message on any topic. He may direct as He did to Phillip when He said, "Go near, and join thyself to this chariot." (Acts 8:29 KJV) He may forbid, as He did Paul, Silas, and Timothy. "And they went through the region of Phrygia and Galatia, having been forbidden by the Holy Spirit to speak the Word in Asia." (Acts 16:6 RSV) He may correct. "And if you leave God's paths and go astray, you will hear a Voice behind you say, 'No, this is the way; walk here.'" (Is. 30:21 TLB) He may even communicate a message about the future. Jesus said, "But when He, the Spirit of truth, comes, He will guide you into all truth. He will not speak on his own; He will speak only what He hears, and He will tell you what is yet to come." (John 16:13 NIV)

Allow me to take the liberty of sharing two personal examples of situations in which I have heard the "voice of the Spirit." The first occurred in 1983. I was the head track coach at Campbell University in North Carolina. We had a rather limited scholarship budget, so I often pursued multi-event athletes so that our team could cover the events with limited personnel. I heard of a young man named Lance Bingham from South Plains Junior College in Levelland, Texas. He had been the 1982 Junior College National runner-up in the decathlon. I contacted him to invite him to consider finishing his collegiate education at Campbell. The first time I spoke with him I learned that he was a committed Christian and so, naturally, my interest in recruiting him increased. I sent him some information about our school and program and then phoned him a second time. I invited him to come for a visit and he said that he would think and pray about it and would answer me when I phoned again.

When I called him the third time, he thanked me for my interest in him, but told me that he had decided to go to college near home and, therefore, there was no point in coming to North Carolina for a visit. I was disappointed, but as I expressed my parting words, a strong "sense" came over me that this was not the end of our relationship. The last thing I said to him was, "This may sound really strange, but I have a strong sense that we are going to work together some day." I don't recall what he said in response, but that was the end of our contact.

After I hung up the phone, I did not run and tell my wife that I had just had a message from God. In fact, I actually remember thinking, "Boy, that was really stupid. Where did that come from?" In the months that followed, I did not know if that message was from the Holy Spirit, another spirit, or simply a thought that I concocted in my own brain. Now, however, I believe that the Spirit spoke to me that day, giving me just a small glimpse of the future.

As I am writing these words, the year is 1998. Lance Bingham is in his third year as assistant track coach at Liberty University, where I serve as head coach. He is my right hand man and best friend. We have experienced many joys and sorrows together. He and I share the same burden to minister to and through athletes to help them become all they can be for the glory of God.

The second personal example that I will relate is a situation that involves you as well as me. In the last chapter I referred to our track team's goal of reading through the entire Bible in 1996. In the process of doing that, the Lord gave me three or four devotional thoughts that I shared with the team at our weekly meetings.

Not long after that devotional series, Laura, one of our most godly female athletes, came to my office to talk to me. She said she had three topics to discuss. After we discussed the first two, she moved to the third. Laura told me was that I should write a book about the things that we had been studying in our team devotions. I responded to the thought with humor and said something like, "Me? Write a book? What? In my spare time?" The thought seemed foreign to me because I had neither the experience nor the desire to write a book, and certainly I didn't have the time. I was engrossed in my coaching responsibilities and in trying to meet the major needs of my large family, which included my wife, our four daughters, and two foster children who had joined our family just over a year earlier. After she left my office, I did not once give it another thought for two weeks.

Then one night I woke up at 2:30 a.m. and could not get back to sleep. For the next three hours I lay quietly in my bed communicating with God. In the process I heard the "voice of the Spirit" telling me to write this book which you are now reading. In my mind, or possibly in my spirit—I do not know—I argued with Him for much of that three hours, giving Him many reasons why I should not attempt this major effort. However, at 5:30 a.m. I got out of bed and went into the kitchen, took out a paper and pen, and in one minute wrote the book title and most of the chapter titles of this book. Like that time on the phone with Lance Bingham, I wondered, Where did that come from? However, this time I knew. The Spirit spoke the outline to me so quickly that I knew God was telling me to do this, and I must simply obey. As I'm writing these words, I have no idea if this will ever be published or whom it may impact. I am not a writer. I'm a coach. I am writing because I heard the "voice of the Spirit." I am writing because I try to live by the things that this book is teaching. God is sovereign. Jesus is Lord. The gifts He gives must be used. The sacrifice of time and energy must be mine. The obedience must be mine. I must not be proud, because it is all from Him. I must not be discouraged, because He is the source. I must use whatever success I can attain to point others to Christ. The lessons of this book are the lessons that I am trying to apply even as I write. And if no one else ever reads this book, you are reading it, and the Spirit of God meant it for you. He somehow guided you here because He wants you to also learn these lessons that He has taught and is teaching me.

It is a wonderful thing to live your life in constant two-way communication with God. I have known a few people who have seemed to do that. I must confess that I am not yet one of them but I hope that someday I will be.

To develop the ability to hear the Spirit when He speaks, it is important that you obey whenever you do hear Him. As I coach I know that when an athlete obeys and applies the things I tell him, it increases my interest in trying to help that athlete. On the contrary, when an athlete fails to pay attention or apply the instructions that I give, I begin to think that there is no point of issuing further instructions. Then I tend to leave the athlete to himself. Perhaps this is also true with the Spirit or perhaps we just dull our hearing when we do not obey. In any case, we will hear better when we obey what we hear.

I conclude this chapter with one final recommendation. Do not desire to live your life by instructions from the voice of the Spirit more than you desire to live by instructions from the Word of God. When you want to hear from God, go to the Word of God. If you live your life according to the Word of God you will not go wrong. The more you know God through the Word of God, the better you will hear and recognize the "voice of the Spirit." "Those who are led by the Spirit of God are sons of God." (Rom. 8:14 NIV) And if we are sons, "then we are heirs—heirs of God and co-heirs with Christ, if indeed we share in His sufferings in order that we may also share in His glory." (Rom. 8:17 NIV) So then, read His Word, hear His voice, obey His instructions, bear your burden and share His glory.

Chapter 14
The Peace of God

It was the most important basketball game of her life. Brenda was a senior on a very good high school team. The team had made it all the way to the state championship for the first time in the school's history. She was not a starter and, in fact, sat on the bench for the majority of every game. Her forte was defense, and when her team was behind by one point with only ten seconds left and the ball in the possession of the opposing team, the coach called time out and put her in.

Brenda could not even remember how it happened, but somehow as time was running out she had managed to steal the ball and had been fouled. The clock read zero, the scoreboard, 56-55, and she had the opportunity to shoot one-and-one. The timeout called by the opposing coach, the encouragement given by her teammates, the shouts of the crowd, and the frenzy in the packed gymnasium were all somehow a blur to her, but when the official handed her the ball she felt the greatest pressure she had ever known.

Yet, she understood the scenario completely. There were three possible outcomes. First, she could miss the first shot and the state championship was lost. She would be the "goat." She would dash the hopes of her coaches, her teammates, her friends, her entire school and even most of the community in which she lived. For the rest of her life she would remember this blown opportunity. Second, she could sink both shots and she would be the hero. She would make a great life-long memory for herself, her team, and their fans. Her name would be in the sport's page headlines. Third, she could hit the first shot and miss the second and the teams would go into overtime. If her team went on to win, her efforts would soon be forgotten and there would likely be another hero. If her team lost, she would share the blame with those who couldn't get the job done in overtime.

As a 50 percent foul shooter and a good math student, she knew that there was 50 percent chance she would be the goat. There was only a 25 percent chance that she would be the hero. Those were the odds without pressure. With the weight of the world on her shoulders, what were the odds? As Brenda raised the ball to launch the first shot, anxiety seemed to overwhelm her. Her fear, turmoil, and stress drained all the joy from the game. She hesitated for two extra long seconds and then, despite her internal warfare, Brenda somehow managed to put up the shot.

So, how did it end? You want to know what happened? Actually, it has ended every possible way. There have been Brendas and Bobs, Marys and Marks who have missed the shot, who have made the first and missed the second and who have made both shots. There have been Joeys and Jennifers, Rachels and Richards who have gotten the hit to win the game and those who have struck out to lose the game. No matter what type of athlete you are or at what level you compete, sooner or later the outcome of a contest will depend on you. Your mistake will result in defeat. Your accomplishment will result in victory. This creates pressure, anxiety, worry, turmoil and stress. The more important the contest, the greater the emotional response.

Occasionally an athlete seems to thrive on this pressure, but usually it is an athlete that has been in similar circumstances many times before and has known the joy of overcoming. However, most athletes are happy if these times of extreme anxiety are rare. Most athletes and coaches prefer to win by a comfortable margin rather than to win by a hair. A close contest has been called a "nail-biter" because of the stress that it creates, and many have been the athletes that have folded under this stress. The athletic term "choking" refers to what an athlete does when he cannot produce under great pressure.

The "surrendered Christian athlete" has a great advantage when it comes to coping with the stress and pressure of athletics. Such an athlete is the only one who can know the "peace of God," that "peace which passeth all understanding." You can have peace in the midst of the storm, a peace which will not only help you to perform better but which will also be a tremendous testimony of the power of God in your life.

Jesus' own disciples struggled to learn this. When they were caught in a storm on the Sea of Galilee and their boat started to fill with water, they began to fear for their lives. Christ, however, was asleep on a pillow in the stern. The Lord of creation was at peace in the storm. "The disciples went and woke Him saying, 'Lord, save us! We're going to drown.' He replied, 'You of little faith, why are you so afraid?' Then He got up and rebuked the winds and the waves, and it was completely calm." (Matt. 8:25-26 NIV)

What a striking contrast there is between the disciples' reaction to the storm and Christ's reaction to the same circumstances. The disciples are focused on the situation surrounding them but Jesus focuses on what is in them, their fear and lack of faith. The disciples see the storm as a negative situation that may take their lives but Christ uses the storm to demonstrate His power and increase their faith. The disciples only experience peace when Jesus calms the sea, but Jesus has peace even in the storm. The storm causes no stress to the Lord. He is God and thereby owns the peace of God. He wants to give it to His disciples.

Jesus said, "Peace I leave with you; my peace I give you. I do not give to you as the world gives. Do not let your hearts be troubled and do not be afraid." (John 14:27 NIV) Later He said, "I have told you these things, so that in me you may have peace. In this world you will have trouble. But take heart! I have overcome the world." (John 16:33 NIV) The trouble, the struggles, the stress that we encounter in this world need not destroy our peace because we can have peace in Christ, "and the peace of God, which transcends all understanding, will guard your hearts and your minds in Christ Jesus." (Philippians 4:7 NIV)

Christ desires for us to enjoy His peace. In this present life it is one of the greatest benefits of knowing the Lord. The secret of the peace of God is in your relationship with God. The more completely you know God the more you will possess of the peace of God. You too can join the Psalmist in truthfully saying, "Yea, though I walk through the valley of the shadow of death, I will fear no evil, for Thou art with me," (Ps. 23: 4) and again, "The Lord is my light and my salvation; whom shall I fear? The Lord is the strength of my life; of whom shall I be afraid?" (Ps. 27:1 KJV)

There are three things that will together impart the gift of God's peace in our lives. First, we must come to know and understand God's sovereignty. Second, we must know and experience God's love. Third, we must know and believe God's promises. The stronger your grasp on these attributes and gifts from God, the greater your peace as you pass through difficult situations.

We began this book with consideration of the sovereignty of God. Yet, it sometimes seems it is easier to believe that God controls the movement of the galaxies than to believe that He controls the outcome if you flip a coin. But the Bible says, "We toss the coin, but it is the Lord who controls its decision." (Prov. 16:33 TLB)

Ephesians 1:11 (NIV) reads, "In Him we were also chosen, having been predestined according to the plan of Him who works out everything in conformity with the purpose of His will...." Not some things, not most things, but **everything** is in conformity with the purpose of His will. This is not to say that everything that happens is God's will. We know that God is "not willing that any should perish, but that all should come to repentance," (II Pet. 3:9) but certainly many are perishing against God's will. When we sin, obviously that is against God's will. Yet, when we sin and reap what we sow, when people reject Christ and perish, though this is not God's will, these things are in conformity with the purpose of God's will. Though God desires that all would be saved, the purpose of Christ's coming was to save those who accepted Him and to condemn those who rejected Him.

Is it any wonder that an omniscient, omnipresent, omnipotent God would be sovereign? Psalm 139 says it so well.

O Lord, You have searched me and You know me. You know when I sit and when I rise; You perceive my thoughts from afar. You discern my going out and my lying down; You are familiar with all my ways. Before a word is on my tongue You know it completely, O Lord. You hem me in— behind and before; You have laid Your hand upon me. Such knowledge is too wonderful for me, too lofty for me to attain. Where can I go from Your Spirit? Where can I flee from Your presence? If I go up to the heavens, You are there; if I make my bed in the depths, You are there. If I rise on the wings of the dawn, if I settle on the far side of the sea, even there Your hand will guide me, Your right hand will hold me fast. If I say, "Surely the darkness will hide me and the light become night around me," even the darkness will not be dark to You; the night will shine like the day, for darkness is as light to You. For You created my inmost being; You knit me together in my mother's womb. I praise You because I am fearfully and wonderfully made; Your works are wonderful, I know that full well. My frame was not hidden from You when I was made in the secret place. When I was woven together in the depths of the earth, Your eyes saw my unformed body. All the days ordained for me were written in Your book before one of them came to be. (NIV)

We have a God who is sovereign, but, in addition to this, God is also love. John wrote, "Dear friends, let us love one another, for love comes from God. Everyone who loves has been born of God and knows God. Whoever does not love does not know God, because God is love." (I John 4:7-8 NIV) And, of course, the most famous verse in the New Testament tells us that "God so loved the world that He gave His only begotten Son, that whosoever believeth in Him should not perish, but have everlasting life." (John 3:16 KJV)

The entire Bible is a love story of God to man, but let me just cite two more verses. In Romans 5:8 Paul says, "But God demonstrates his own love for us in this: While we were still sinners, Christ died for us." Jesus said, "Greater love has no one than this, that he lay down his life for his friends." (John 15:13 NIV)

If we believe that God is sovereign and in control of all the things that happen in our lives and if we "grasp how wide and long and high and deep is the love of Christ, and (to) know this love that surpasses knowledge…" (Eph. 3:18-19 NIV), those things in themselves should be sufficient to give God's peace. Yet, understanding how prone humans are to act on feelings and to forget in crises what they know and believe in the calm, God in His Word has given us promises that we can hold on to as we go through the storms of life.

The Scriptures are full of promises that comfort us, that encourage us, and that assure us that our loving Father is in control. The Bible gives us promises that apply to the present, promises for the future of this earthly life, and promises for the life to come. Let's look at just a few of these wonderful promises.

For the present, if we know the Lord we are assured of our position in Christ. Paul wrote, "Therefore, there is now no condemnation for those who are in Christ Jesus…." (Rom. 8:1 NIV) Jesus said of us, His sheep, "…no one can snatch them out of my Father's hand." (John 10:29b NIV) He also said, "Come unto Me, all you who are weary and burdened, and I will give you rest. Take My yoke upon you, and learn from me, for I am gentle and humble in heart, and you will find rest for your souls. For My yoke is easy and my burden is light." (Matt. 11:28-30 NIV) Then, also for the present, we have the Spirit's well-known assurance through Paul that "… in all things God works for the good of those who love Him, who have been called according to His purpose." (Romans 8:28 NIV)

God's promises for our future both on earth and into eternity are exciting. Jesus said, "My Father will honor the one who serves Me." (John 12:26b NIV) He also promised, "…everyone who has left houses or brothers or sisters or father or mother or children or fields for My sake will receive a hundred times as much and will inherit eternal life." (Matt. 19:29 NIV) The Word also tells us, "No eye has seen, no ear heard, no mind has conceived what God has prepared for those who love Him." (I Cor. 2:9 NIV) Again we read, "He who did not spare His own Son, but gave Him up for us all— how will He not also, along with Him, graciously give us all things? Who shall separate us from the love of Christ?" (Rom. 8:32, 35a NIV)

No matter what may befall you in this life, Christ comforts you, if you are His disciple, with these words, "Do not let your heart be troubled. Trust in God; trust also in Me. In My Father's house are many rooms; if it were not so, I would have told you. I am going there to prepare a place for you. And if I go and prepare a place for you, I will come back and take you to be with Me that you also may be where I am." (John 14:1-3 NIV) The Lord created this earth and heaven in six days. What has He prepared for you in the past 2000 years?

Therefore, "do not be anxious about anything, but in everything, by prayer and petition, with thanksgiving, present your requests to God. And the peace of God, which transcends all understanding, will guard your hearts and your minds in Christ Jesus." (Phil. 4: 6-7 NIV)

Chapter 15
The Power of Prayer

"Set - Red - 92 - Red - 92 - Hit." The quarterback grabbed the ball from the center and turning, pressed it firmly into the arms of the charging running back. A small hole opened up in the defensive line and the back was quickly through it. Once in the secondary, he cut to the left, switching the ball to his left hand, and headed for the first down marker. Just before reaching the sideline, he made an amazing move and two would-be tacklers flew by as he reversed his field and headed for pay dirt. As the home crowd roared, he charged into the end zone. Before any visible celebration, he dropped down on one knee, bowing his head for a short thanksgiving prayer. Immediately, three yellow flags were in the air and whistles blew signifying a penalty. Then the official announced, "Fifteen yard penalty on the ensuing kick-off." His violation? Praying in the end zone.

This may well have been a real occurrence if the NCAA had imposed the unsportsman-like conduct rule interpretation that they proposed in 1995. The National Collegiate Athletic Association told the football establishment that it would prohibit prayer on the football field. Any player who felt the need to bend his knee after a touchdown would be assessed a fifteen-yard penalty on the ensuing kick-off. A second infraction would make the player eligible for ejection. The NCAA rescinded the rule when four collegiate football players and Coach Sam Rutigliano from Liberty University filed suit against the NCAA charging that the rule violated religious freedom rights.

What was the reason for such a rule? Was it because praying gives an athlete or team an advantage? Was it because the power of prayer is obvious to everyone and the NCAA didn't want people who pray to be able to take advantage of this extra power? Obviously, not! In fact, it has been my observation that there is no direct relationship between prayer at athletic contests and the outcome of that contest. It appears to me that prayer at athletic events is most often motivated by fear. Fear of a coming trial draws most people to prayer. If you are a student taking a test for which you have prepared well or taking a test for which you are unprepared, when are you more likely to pray? Even in the public school setting where open prayer is curtailed, people will pray when tragedies, which they don't know how to handle, strike. When people sense the need for power outside of themselves, that's when they feel a need to pray.

With an athletic department committed to glorifying the Lord, Liberty University frequently has prayer before and after athletic events. However, often at the start of large cross-country races drawing primarily secular schools, the starting line looks like a revival meeting. Nearly all the teams are huddled together for team prayers before the race. From their conduct during and after the race, I suspect that most of these athletes have no personal relationship with God. Nevertheless, as they are anxious and apprehensive about the soon-coming struggle and pain, they are eager to pray, to attempt to call upon some unknown power.

But if prayer does not make the runner run better, the swimmer swim better, the basketball player shoot better, or the golfer putt better, what is the power of prayer? Why bother to pray? Why invest time in prayer?

There are many reasons that Christians should pray and that surrendered Christians will pray. First of all, even if there were no power in prayer, we should still pray simply because God's Word commands us to pray. We not only have Christ's example and the disciples' example in prayer, but we are also directly commanded to pray. We are told to pray without ceasing (I Th. 5:17), at all times

(Eph. 6:18), always (Luke 18:1), steadfastly (Col. 4:2) and constantly (Rom. 12:12). The Bible tells us to pray for the peace of Jerusalem (Ps. 122:6), to pray for those who persecute us (Matt. 5:44) or abuse us (Luke 6:28), to pray for everyone including kings and all who are in high places (I Tim.2: 1-2), and to pray if we are in trouble (James 5:13). Paul instructs us to devote ourselves to prayer (Col. 4:2) and exhorts us, "Do not be anxious about anything, but in everything, by prayer and petition, with thanksgiving, present your requests to God." (Phil. 4:6) Samuel indicated that it is possible to sin by not praying when he said, "As for me, far be it from me that I should sin against the Lord by failing to pray for you." (I Sam. 12:23) Therefore, if we are obedient, we will pray.

Second, however, is the wonderful truth that prayer is able to change things. You can affect the outcome of a situation by praying about it. Prayer can serve to bring action from Almighty God. Joshua prayed and the sun stood still in the sky for an entire day. (Josh. 10:12-13) Samson prayed and his great strength returned so that he pulled down the temple of Dagon. (Judges 16) Hannah prayed and God opened her barren womb and gave her a son. (I Sam. 1) Elijah prayed and rain ceased in Israel for three and a half years. He prayed again and the rains returned. (I Kings 17-18) Isaiah prayed and the shadow moved backward ten steps on the stairway of Ahaz. (II Kings 20:11) Jonah prayed and God rescued him from the belly of the fish. (Jonah 2) There is a multitude of examples of answered prayers from the Scriptures. We would also have little difficulty finding examples of answered prayers in the lives of Christians today. One of the assurances that Christians have of the reality of their faith lies in their answered prayers.

However, it is obvious that not all prayers bring immediate, situation changing action from God. If right at this moment you ask God for an immediate ten million dollars, your doorbell will probably not ring with the Publisher's Clearinghouse Sweepstakes team at your door. And if two athletes, even Christian athletes, competing against each other both pray for victory, one will not have his request granted. Does that mean that God picks and chooses which prayers He will answer and which He will ignore? Is the power in prayer like power in old, wet firecrackers—most of them are duds, but once in awhile one may go off? Isn't there any means by which we can be assured that our prayers will be answered?

The reality is that most prayers are not answered. However, the reason is not God's inability or disinterest, and it is not because He randomly selects just certain prayers to answer. Rather, it is because most people do not meet the requirements that are necessary to get their prayers answered. There are several conditions that must be met if we expect God to respond to our prayers. These conditions were the same during Old Testament times as they are during the current church age. The Lord outlined these conditions for King Solomon in II Chronicles 7:14 and He also addressed each of the conditions when He taught His disciples to pray. The Lord told Solomon, "...if my people, who are called by my name, will humble themselves, and pray and seek my face and turn from their wicked ways, then will I hear from heaven and will forgive their sin and will heal their land."

The first condition necessary to get your prayers answered I will call the family condition. The Lord said, "if **my** people, who are called by **my** name...." This promise is spoken to people who belong to God, people who are members of His family. Jesus began the model prayer with the words, "Our Father." In order to gain the right to expect God to answer your prayers, you must belong to Him. "If anyone does not have the Spirit of Christ, he does not belong to Christ," (Rom. 8:9 NIV) but "those who are led by the Spirit of God are sons of God." (Rom. 8:14 NIV) If we are His sons, He is, as Jesus said, "Our Father," and, just as you bear your earthly father's name, so as God's children we are "called by His name."

The second condition is the position condition. We must recognize our position before God, that is, who we are and who God is. Solomon was told, "if my people...will humble themselves...."

Humility begins when we observe our weakness and His power. Humility increases when we recognize our sinfulness and His holiness. Humility arrives when we comprehend our unworthiness and His great love. In lessons on prayer it is taught that praise is an important and necessary part of prayer. Praise will result as a natural response to the recognition of who God is and who we are. In the Lord's Prayer Jesus continued, "hallowed be Thy name," and concluded, "for Thine is the kingdom and the power and the glory forever." These words, if they are fully comprehended, can only be truthfully spoken from a position of humility.

The third condition is the petition condition. Webster's dictionary defines prayer as "a humble entreaty addressed to God, a request made to God." We must ask, petition, pray. God wants us to ask Him to supply our needs. As we saw earlier, Paul exhorts us in Philippians to, "in everything, by prayer and petition, with thanksgiving, **present your requests** to God." (Phil. 4: 6 NIV) James said, "You do not have, because you do not ask God." (James 4: 2 NIV) God delights to give us gifts and to grant our requests. Jesus said, "If you, then, though you are evil, know how to give good gifts to your children, how much more will your Father in heaven give good gifts to those who ask Him?" (Matt. 7:11 NIV)

In his model prayer Jesus asked, or made petition, for six things. Imagine that you could ask for six things, any six things, knowing that those requests would be granted. For what would you ask? Can you ask for anything? The answer to that question might be yes and it might be no. If you come to God, humbly, recognizing who He is and who you are, you will not come with a Christmas wish list of what you want. You will not look at God as a magic genie that you beckon to grant your wishes. James continues, "When you ask, you do not receive, because you ask with wrong motives, that you may spend what you get on your own pleasures." (James 4:3 NIV) Jesus said, "If you have faith and do not doubt…if you believe, you will receive whatever you ask for in prayer." (Matt. 21:21-22 NIV) In order to have faith in God, you must know God. As your knowledge of God increases, your understanding of His will also increases. The beloved disciple, John, wrote, "This is the confidence we have in approaching God: that if we ask anything according to His will, He hears us. And if we know that He hears us—whatever we ask— we know that we have what we asked of Him." (I John 5:14-15 NIV) So, if our request is according to the will of God, we can know that it will be granted.

Let's examine the six requests that Jesus made in the "Lord's Prayer." (1) "May Thy kingdom come." Christ had come to establish this kingdom, first of all in the hearts of men, so surely this request was according to God's will. (2) "May Thy will be done, on earth as it is in heaven." Here He prays specifically for God's will to be done on earth. (3) "Give us this day our daily bread." The prayer asks not for a year's supply which could be stockpiled for security, not for a month's supply which could help provide peace of mind, not even a week's supply which might remove a little worry, but only for the bread necessary for that day. The request is not only for bread for the individual offering the prayer but also for others with whom the person praying is associated. Surely this request is according to God's will since Christ taught his followers not to worry about food, for God even feeds the birds of the air which are much less valuable than people. (4) "Forgive us our debts…." The Father sent Christ to die to make forgiveness available to us, so surely He wants us to request that forgiveness. Here again the prayer concerns more than just the one praying as it says, "Forgive us" instead of "Forgive me." (5) "Lead us not into temptation." "God cannot be tempted by evil, neither does He tempt anyone; but each one is tempted when, by his own evil desire, he is dragged away and enticed." (James 1:13-14 NIV) God does allow you to follow a pathway upon which you will encounter temptations, but, "God is faithful; He will not let you be tempted beyond what you can bear. But when you are tempted, He will also provide a way out so that you can stand up under it." (I Cor. 10:13 NIV) Praying to avoid and resist temptation is surely according to God's will. Finally, (6) "Deliver us from evil." Peter later wrote, "Your enemy the devil prowls around like a roaring lion looking for someone to devour." (I Peter 5:8 NIV) Evil can destroy even a Christian's life and certainly his testimony. God does not want that to happen, so He is pleased when we pray for deliverance. Notice that requests 5 and 6 are also plural requests, seeking deliverance for a group.

Six requests, but none have any hint of selfishness or desire for personal gain. All are surely according to God's will, so when requested from a properly prepared and positioned heart, all will be granted. True, sometimes it is difficult to know if your request is according to God's will. Sometimes it seems impossible to know God's will when we are making requests. Paul recognized this when he wrote, "In the same way, the Spirit helps us in our weakness. We do not know what we ought to pray for, but the Spirit Himself intercedes for us with groans that words cannot express. And He who searches our hearts knows the mind of the Spirit, because the Spirit intercedes for the saints in accordance with God's will." (Rom. 8:26-27 NIV) If you know your request is not according to God's will, don't ask. If you believe your request might be according to God's will, bring your request to God. Even Jesus Christ asked for something which was not according to the Father's will when He prayed that the "cup" of crucifixion might be removed from Him. However, He qualified His request with, "Not My will, but Thine be done."

A fourth condition, given in Chronicles, is necessary to get God to answer your prayers. "If my people...seek my face...then will I hear...." What does it mean to seek God's face? Moses, with whom God communicated as a man to a man, asked to see God's face. God told him, "You cannot see my face, for no one may see Me and live." (Ex. 33:20) Moses wanted to "see God's face" because he had a personal relationship with God. It is this relationship, this face to face relationship, that we must seek. If "you seek the Lord your God, you will find Him if you look for Him with all your heart and with all your soul." (Deut. 4:29 NIV) In the book of Jeremiah, the Lord declared, "For I know the plans I have for you, plans to prosper you and not to harm you, plans to give you hope and a future. Then you will call upon me, and I will listen to you. You will seek Me and find Me when you seek Me with all your heart." (Jer. 29: 11-13 NIV) God was speaking to Israel, but these words can be applied to you as well.

As we seek God, as we cultivate our relationship with Him through Bible study and prayer, as we come to know Him better and as we grow to love Him more, our lives will increasingly conform to His will and our prayers will also conform to His will. Then God's words in Psalm 91 will apply to us, "Because he loves me," says the Lord, "I will rescue him; I will protect him, for he acknowledges my name. He will call upon me (pray), and I will answer him; I will be with him in trouble, I will deliver him and honor him." (Ps. 91:14-15 NIV)

When in the Lord's Prayer we pray, "Thy kingdom come, Thy will be done, on earth as it is in heaven," we are seeking God's face. We are recognizing that His ways are above our ways, His thoughts above our thoughts, and His will superior to our wills. We are expressing our faith in Him. As we seek Him and find Him and learn to trust Him, we begin to desire His will for our lives more than we desire our own will. We surrender our will to His will and become "surrendered Christians."

Finally, a fifth condition is required for assurance of God's answer to a prayer. "If my people...turn from their wicked ways...then will I hear from heaven, and forgive their sin, and heal their land." This is the righteousness condition.

Jesus' brother, James, wrote, "the prayer of a righteous man is powerful and effective." (James 5:16b NIV) Proverbs says that "The Lord is far from the wicked but he hears the prayers of the righteous." (Prov. 15:29 NIV) The apostle Peter restates this truth in these words, "For the eyes of the Lord are on the righteous and His ears are attentive to their prayer." (I Pet. 3:12 NIV) The beloved disciple, John, confirmed this stating, "Dear friends, if our hearts do not condemn us, we have confidence before God and receive from Him anything we ask, because we obey his commands and do what pleases Him." (I John 3:21-22 NIV) The Psalmist wrote, "If I had cherished sin in my heart, the Lord would not have listened; but God has surely listened and heard my voice in prayer." (Ps. 66:18 NIV)

Recognize, however, that the righteousness requirement is not a perfection requirement. We know that "all have sinned and come short of the glory of God," but we must repent and our sins must be confessed, forgiven, and covered by the blood of the Perfect Lamb. We must "turn from our wicked ways." God will forgive our sins and give us a pure heart when we repent and confess our sins, provided that we fulfill one other requirement. "For if you forgive men when they sin against you, your heavenly Father will also forgive you. But if you do not forgive men their sins, your Father in heaven will not forgive your sins." (Matt. 6:14-15 NIV)

This is the reason the Lord taught the disciples to pray, "Forgive us our debts as we forgive our debtors." This point cannot be over emphasized. No matter how sincere your sorrow for your sins or how stirring your confession, you will not have your sins forgiven, you will not fulfill the righteousness requirement, and you will not have your prayers answered if you refuse to forgive the brother or sister who has wronged you.

Jesus offered a powerful illustration of this truth in His parable of the unmerciful servant found in Matthew 18. Recall that the king forgave his servant a huge debt but that servant later refused to forgive a small debt from a fellow servant. Instead he had him thrown in prison. When the king learned of this, he "called the servant in. 'You wicked servant,' he said, 'I cancelled all that debt of yours because you begged me to. Shouldn't you have had mercy on your fellow servant just as I had mercy on you?' In anger the master turned him over to the jailers to be tortured, until he should pay all he owed." (Matt. 18:32-34 NIV) Then Jesus said, "This is how my heavenly Father will treat each of you unless you forgive your brother from your heart." So, you must forgive others if you are to experience the forgiveness that will allow you to meet the righteousness condition.

If you meet all the necessary conditions, you can expect God to answer your prayers. You then have at your disposal the most powerful force in the world. As my pastor often says, "Prayer can do anything God can do, and since God can do anything, prayer is omnipotent." The power of prayer is the same as the power of God. Prayer can change any situation and solve any problem.

So then, we pray out of obedience and we pray to effect changes in the world. In addition, prayer also serves one more important purpose. Prayer can change not only things but it can also change the "pray-er." The very act of praying, of recognizing God's character, of humbling yourself, of spending time communing with God, of confessing your sins and seeking His face will help conform your will to God's will. There is a power that you can personally receive from prayer that will strengthen and equip you to accomplish God's will. We see a vivid example of this by again examining Jesus Christ's prayer in the Garden of Gethsemane. Knowing of His soon coming persecution and crucifixion, Jesus was greatly troubled and in great anguish. "His soul was overwhelmed with sorrow to the point of death" so that "His sweat was like drops of blood falling to the ground." (Luke 22:44) In His humanity He asked the Father to remove the coming trial from Him but concluded, "Yet, not my will, but Yours be done." When He rose from prayer, Jesus went to meet His betrayer, and with great strength of character and with no apparent fear, He accepted God's will and "for the joy that was set before Him endured the cross, scorning its shame…." He got on His knees to plead for His own will, but arose focused on the Father's will. A similar transformation can take place as you pray today.

Prayer is the lifeblood of the Christian. It is the process of teaming up with God to accomplish His purposes. Prayer is the difference between a nominal Christian and an anointed Christian. The depth of one's prayer life will determine the height of his spiritual walk. God created man to have fellowship with Him and prayer is the primary means to that fellowship. Why then do so many Christians spend so little time in prayer? Many professing Christians don't even pray for one minute a day.

The surrendered Christian athlete must have a vibrant prayer life. He can say with David, "I call to God, and the Lord saves me. Evening, morning and noon I cry out in distress, and He hears my voice. He ransoms me unharmed from the battle waged against me, even though many oppose me. God, who is enthroned forever, will hear them and afflict them.... (Ps. 55: 16-19 NIV) Cast your cares on the Lord and He will sustain you; He will never let the righteous fall.... But as for me, I trust in You." (Ps. 55: 22, 23b NIV)

You must train hard to become the best athlete that you can be. You must pray hard to become the powerful Christian you can be. Reflect on the answer to these two questions. If you trained as much as you pray, what kind of athlete would you be? If you prayed as much as you train, what kind of Christian would you be?

I close this chapter with a true story illustrating the power of prayer. Have you ever heard how Dwight L. Moody became a worldwide evangelist? After the great fire in Chicago, Mr. Moody stayed in Chicago long enough to get money together to feed the poor and to provide a new building for his own work, and then he went to England for a rest.

He did not intend to preach at all, but wanted to hear some of the great preachers on the other side of the water…Spurgeon, George Muller, and others. He was invited to preach one Sunday in a Congregational church in the north of London, of which a Mr. Lessey was the pastor. He accepted the invitation. On Sunday morning, as he preached, he had great difficulty.

As he told the story to me [R. A. Torrey] many years afterwards, he said, "I had no power, no liberty; it seemed like pulling a heavy train up a steep grade, and as I preached I said to myself, 'What a fool I was to consent to preach. I came here to hear others, and here I am preaching.' As I drew to the close of my sermon, I had a sense of relief that I was so near through, and then the thought came to me, 'Well, I've got to do it again tonight.'

I tried to get Mr. Lessey to release me from preaching that night, but he would not consent. I went to the evening service with a heavy heart. But I had not been preaching long when it seemed as if the powers of an unseen world had fallen upon that audience. As I drew to the close of my sermon, I got courage to draw the net. I asked all that would then and there accept Christ to rise, and about 500 people arose to their feet. I thought there must be some mistake, so I asked them to sit down, and then I said, 'There will be an after-meeting in the vestry, and if any of you really will accept Christ, meet the pastor and me in the vestry.'

There was a door at each side of the pulpit into the vestry and people began to stream through these doors into the vestry, and I turned to Mr. Lessey and said, 'Mr. Lessey, who are these people?' He replied, 'I do not know.' 'Are they your people?' 'Some of them are.' 'Are they Christians?' 'Not as far as I know.' We went into the vestry and I repeated the invitation in a stronger form, and they all rose again. I still thought there must be some mistake, and I asked them to be seated, and repeated the invitation in a still stronger form, and again they all arose. I still thought there must be some mistake and I said to the people, 'I am going to Ireland tomorrow, but your pastor will be here tomorrow night. If you really mean what you have said here tonight, meet him here.'

After I reached Ireland, I received a telegram from Mr. Lessey saying there were more people out Monday night than on Sunday night. 'A revival has broken out in our church and you must come back and help me.'

Mr. Moody hurried back from Dublin to London and held a series of meetings in Mr. Lessey's church that added hundreds of people to the churches of North London, and that is what led to the invitation that took him over to England later for the great work that stirred the whole world.

After Mr. Moody had told me that story, I said, 'Mr. Moody, someone must have been praying.' 'Oh,' he said, 'did I not tell you that? That is the point of the whole story. There were two sisters in that church, one of whom was bedridden; the other one heard me that Sunday morning. She went home and said to her sister, 'Who do you suppose preached for us this morning?' The sister replied, 'I do not know.' Then she said, 'Guess,' and the other sister guessed all the men Mr. Lessey was in the habit of exchanging pulpits with, but her sister said, 'No.' Then her sister asked, 'Who did preach this morning?' And she replied, 'Mr. Moody, of Chicago.' No sooner had she said it than her sister turned as pale as death and said, 'What! Mr. Moody of Chicago? I have read of him in an American paper and I have been praying to God to send him to London, and to send him to our church. If I had known he was to preach this morning I would have eaten no breakfast and I would have spent the whole morning in fasting and prayer. Now, sister, go out, lock the door, do not let anyone come to see me, do not let them send me any dinner. I am going to spend the whole afternoon and evening in fasting and prayer!'"

And pray she did. And God heard, and answered.

Chapter 16
The Futility of Faith

It was the "team of destiny." At least that is what everyone believed. That name was first assigned to the hockey team by the sportswriter of the local newspaper after they won their fifth straight game of the season. The squad did not seem to be exceptionally talented, but somehow they managed to win each of their first four games by just one goal. In the fifth game, the high school age boys had fallen behind by a score of three to zero with only three minutes left to play. Somehow the club managed to score three times in those final minutes, forcing overtime. They grabbed the victory with a fourth goal as the time expired in overtime. It started then to appear that this team could not lose. The coach claimed that "Team of Destiny" title and used it to build tremendous confidence in his young players. They continued to win games, one after another, although without any of the results of a dominant team. In fact, most of their victories were by only one goal, but with each passing victory the players' faith grew stronger and stronger. They believed that they could not lose.

After fifteen straight victories the "Team of Destiny" was in the provincial championship game. The coach reminded them of the amazing season they were concluding. He reminded them of the repeated times they had snatched victory from the clutches of their opponents. He reminded them of their "destiny." Every player on that team knew they would win. They knew it would be a struggle, but they knew they would be victorious. They had total faith in their ability to get the job done. There was no fear and no doubt, only excitement.

They were right; the game was a battle. At the end of regulation, the score was tied at one apiece. That was no surprise to the Team of Destiny. They'd been there before and they loved the drama. They all knew what the outcome would be. The overtime was even more intense – body checks everywhere, four shots on goal for each team. With twenty seconds left the opposition was pressing hard for a score when Sam, the season leading scorer from that undefeated team, suddenly stole a pass and broke away down the ice. As the clock ticked to single digits he set up for a slap shot from five-meters with only the goalie in the way of victory. His teammates prepared for the celebration as Sam slapped a lightning-fast shot toward the goal. The goalie never touched it, but the puck bounced off the side post of the goal right to the nearest defender who had followed the play. He scooped it in and, as the clocked showed three seconds, he fired a shot the length of the ice. Everyone on the ice was taken by surprise and was out of position. Unbelievably, the puck squeezed through the bodies and plunged into the back of the net. The "Team of Destiny" had lost. The players were stunned with disbelief. What had happened to their destiny? Their unwavering faith had proved futile.

Unquestionably, confidence plays a major role in athletic success. Believing you will accomplish something predisposes you toward success whereas believing you cannot be successful predisposes you toward failure. An athlete or team rarely accomplishes something that they believe is impossible. Belief or faith is an important element of success. However, faith in itself is futile. Faith is only of value when that faith is placed in something that is real or true.

If you sit on a chair that you believe will hold you, it does not hold you because you believe it will but because it is designed with enough strength to hold you. If it is not strong enough, it will collapse, even though you have perfect faith, believing 100 percent that it will hold you. Or if you phone a friend and you believe that you dialed the right number, it is not your belief that makes the connection, but it is the actual number that you dialed that determines how the switching system works and whose phone rings. If the number is wrong, you will not reach your friend.

In Mark 5 we read about a woman who had been suffering with a bleeding condition for twelve years. Believing that if she could just touch Jesus' garment she would be healed, that woman pushed her way toward Christ. When she finally got close enough, she reached out and touched His cloak and "immediately her bleeding stopped and she felt in her body that she was freed from her suffering." (Mark 5: 29 NIV) Jesus knew what happened and asked, "Who touched Me?" With great fear the woman confessed, but then Jesus said to her, "Daughter, your faith has healed you. Go in peace and be freed from your suffering." "Your faith has healed you." Does this not imply that it was indeed her faith that provided the power for the healing? Is this not an evidence of the power of faith?

Actually, closer inspection gives the answer in verse 30, which reads, "At once Jesus realized that power had gone out of Him." So, in reality then, it was not the power of her faith but the power of Jesus that healed her. Why then did Jesus tell her that her faith had healed her? Certainly her faith had played a role in her healing. In fact, her faith was the first step of the process that led to her healing. Her belief that Jesus could heal her caused her to take the actions that put her into the position to claim the reality of Jesus' saving and healing power. If Jesus did not have the power to heal her, her faith would have been in vain. That is why James writes, "Faith without works is dead." Real faith, living faith, leads to action and the action leads to the desired result if that faith is in something that is real. James asks, "What good is it, my brothers, if a man claims to have faith but has no deeds? Can such faith save him?" (James 2: 14 NIV) "Show me your faith without deeds, and I will show you my faith by what I do." (James 3: 18 NIV)

A faith that does not lead to action is a faith that is of no value, a faith without life, a dead faith. If you believe that a particular stock on the stock exchange is going to go up in the next month, and therefore you buy that stock, when your belief is correct and the stock does rise, that true belief is of value to you because you acted on it. If, however, you did not buy the stock even though you really believed it would go up, that belief turned out to be of no value to you because you did not act upon it. Your faith without action was worthless or futile.

In the "Faith Hall of Fame" in Hebrews 11, each Old Testament saint that is commended for his faith is cited for the action that resulted because of his faith. "By faith Noah...built an ark." "By faith Abraham...went...." By faith Moses...chose...." And so on it goes. Faith in itself does not please God, but the action that arises from true faith pleases God and receives His reward.

Successful faith, faith that is not futile, faith that serves to accomplish something good, is not something that we muster up to make us perform better or accomplish our goals, but rather it is merely the ability to recognize reality. Recognizing reality you naturally believe that reality. If you correctly realize that the chair is strong enough to hold you, you will of course have the confidence, or faith, to sit in the chair. Faith in God involves knowing God. It is impossible to get to know God without developing faith in Him. Because of who He is, because of His nature and character, there are certain things that He will do and we can count on those things. This is the reason that Hebrews 11:6 tells us, "...without faith it is impossible to please God, because anyone who comes to Him must believe that He exists and that He rewards those who earnestly seek Him." Notice that this passage does not say that faith pleases God. Rather it says that you cannot please God without faith. What pleases God is the action which results when you believe that "God is, and that He is a rewarder of them that diligently seek Him." The action of coming to Him and seeking Him pleases Him.

Jesus commended the faith of a Gentile centurion in Luke 7:9 saying, "I tell you, I have not found such great faith even in Israel." What was this faith that was beyond any that Jesus saw in the Jews?

The centurion was requesting healing for a suffering servant of his who was about to die, but many had come requesting healing from Jesus. However, before Jesus reached the sick man, the centurion sent this message, "Lord, don't trouble yourself, for I do not deserve to have you come under my roof. That is why I did not even consider myself worthy to come to you. But say the word and my servant will be healed. For I myself am a man under authority with soldiers under me. I tell this one, 'Go,' and he goes; and that one, 'Come,' and he comes. I say to my servant, 'Do this,' and he does it."

This centurion somehow recognized more of Jesus' authority and power than anyone else in Israel. He more completely knew the reality of the statement that Jesus later made, "All authority in heaven and on earth has been given to me." (Matt. 28:17) He believed that Jesus could heal without even being present, and this was in fact true, for we read in verse 10, "Then the men who had been sent returned to the house and found the servant well." His faith was merely his recognition of reality, the reality of Christ's power, and his actions were a result of that recognition.

How much of the reality of God's power do you recognize? How much of God's will do you understand? How much about the character and heart of God do you comprehend? How well do you know God? As you increase your knowledge of God, your faith will correspondingly increase. That faith will not be futile but will be of great value because it will lead to actions based upon truth, works that will accomplish His purposes, works that will count for all eternity. Do you want to become a man or woman of great faith? Then become a man or woman who knows God.

Chapter 17
The Blessings of God

How would you like to have God's blessing on your athletic life? How about God's blessing on your entire life? I have often told other coaches, "It is impossible to out-coach or out-recruit the blessing of God," and I know that is true. What will you be able to accomplish if you get God's blessing? In this chapter I would like to show you, from the Holy Scriptures, how you can have the blessing of God upon your life. We will discover what you need to do to make certain, to be 100 percent sure, that the blessing of the Almighty God is upon you and upon whatever you do.

However, before we do that, I'd like you to think about what God's blessing means to you. Imagine for a few moments what would take place in your athletic endeavors during the coming year if God poured out His richest blessing upon your efforts. Let your imagination run free as you contemplate accomplishing one goal after another. What would unfold for you during the coming year? What levels of performance would you and your team reach in that year? Don't rush through this exercise. Take a few minutes to daydream about this. Imagine that anything you can dream up will occur this year. What will you accomplish? Now, take this exercise one step further. Imagine that this year of blessing is not only upon your athletic life but also upon your entire life. What else will happen to you? What will happen financially? What will happen socially? How would you feel as you moved into this coming year of God's richest blessing?

There is no question whether God wants to bless you if you are His child. The words we read from Matthew 7:11 in chapter 15 on prayer are similarly repeated in Luke 11. Jesus said, "Which of you fathers, if your son asks for a fish, will give him a snake instead? Or if he asks for an egg, will give him a scorpion? If you then, though you are evil, know how to give good gifts to your children, how much more will your Father in heaven give the Holy Spirit to those who ask Him?" (Luke 11: 11-13 NIV) "He who did not spare His own Son, but gave Him up for us all—how will He not also, along with Him, graciously give us all things?" (Rom. 8: 32 NIV) He wants to bless you.

There should also be no question about God's ability to bless you, for He is the sovereign, Almighty, Creator and sustainer of the universe. He spoke the universe into existence and controls it by His power. Surely He can control the things you would like Him to control. In the words of Paul paraphrased in the Living Bible, "Now glory be to God who by His mighty power at work within us is able to do far more than we would ever dare to ask or even dream of— infinitely beyond our highest prayers, desires, thoughts or hopes." (Eph. 3:20) He is able to bless you.

So then, if God is willing and able, what must you do to receive God's blessing upon you and upon your life? What must you do so that it can be said of you, "He is indeed blessed by God"?

One day on a mountainside, Jesus answered this question for His disciples, for the crowd gathered around Him, and for us. He said, "Blessed are the poor in spirit, for theirs is the kingdom of heaven." Notice that He did not say, "Blessed will be the poor in spirit," but rather, He spoke in the present tense. If you **are** poor in spirit, you **are** blessed. "Poor in spirit" is not a phrase we regularly use today. The Modern Language translation says, "Blessed are they who know their spiritual poverty…." Spiritual poverty is in contrast to spiritual pride and self-sufficiency. This is illustrated by the difference between the Pharisee and publican that Christ spoke of in Luke 18: 10-14. The one who understands his own depravity and spiritual need and his own inability to meet that need, the one who therefore knows his need for a savior and his dependency upon that Savior, he is blessed, and his "is the kingdom of heaven." Again, it is not "his **will be** the kingdom of heaven" but "his **is**...." The things that are a part of the kingdom of heaven belong to us when we are poor in spirit. "Praise be to the God and Father of our Lord Jesus Christ, who has blessed us in the heavenly realms with every spiritual blessing in Christ." (Eph. 1:3 NIV) We cannot yet fully comprehend this and we cannot in this life fully experience it, but we who know Christ **are blessed** "with every spiritual blessing in Christ." We have an "inheritance that can never perish, spoil or fade—kept in heaven for (us), who through faith are shielded by God's power until the coming of the salvation that is ready to be revealed in the last time." (I Peter 1: 4-5 NIV)

If you have a million dollars in the bank, you are a millionaire even when your wallet is empty. Although at times the wallet of life down here may seem empty, the bank in the heavenly realms always holds your great fortune.

Christ went on to describe seven other groups of people who have God's blessing. The next group actually appears, on first inspection, to be lacking God's blessing. "Blessed are those who mourn...." The phrase itself seems to present a contradiction. How can people who are mourning or grieving be also experiencing the blessing of God?

The truth is that there is much about which to grieve in this world. It is all the result of sin. The Christian has a genuine sorrow for his own sin and he is grieved by the knowledge that his sins insult a Holy God. In addition, sin has brought pain, sorrow and death to this world and every person experiences these. The Christian who obeys Christ's command to love his neighbor as he loves himself will mourn or grieve with his neighbor who is suffering even though at that moment things may be going well for him. Even reading in the newspaper about a tragedy on the other side of the world will bring grief to the heart of a Christian who has the mind of Christ. Since everyone is his neighbor and since someone is always suffering, the Christian is one who mourns. Until Christ returns, sin will bring grief to mankind and those who belong to Jesus will mourn. Paul said, "…we ourselves, who have the firstfruits of the Spirit, groan inwardly as we wait eagerly for our adoption as sons, the redemption of our bodies." (Rom. 8:23 NIV)

Jesus completed the statement, "Blessed are those who mourn, for they will be comforted." (Matt. 5: 4 NIV) The Old Testament prophet, Isaiah, said of Jesus, "He will swallow up death in victory; and the Lord God will wipe away all tears from off all faces; and the rebuke of His people shall He take away from off all the earth: for the Lord hath spoken it." (Is. 25:8) So when the heartaches and disappointments of life cause you to mourn, remember that you are thereby placed among the group that Jesus called "blessed."

The third group of the "blessed are the meek, for they will inherit the earth." A parallel verse is found in Psalm 37, verse 11. "But the meek will inherit the land and enjoy great peace." The NIV notes give this definition of meek: those who humbly acknowledge their dependence on the goodness and grace of God and betray no arrogance toward their fellowman. Unfortunately "meekness" is not common among athletes today but if you want God's blessing, pursue meekness.

Fourth, "blessed are those who hunger and thirst for righteousness, for they will be filled." Jesus proclaims a blessing on those who earnestly desire to be righteous, those who obey His command to "seek first His [the heavenly Father's] kingdom and His righteousness." (Matt. 6:33) Paul twice exhorts Timothy to "pursue righteousness." (I Tim. 6:11, 2 Tim. 2:22) "Hunger and thirst" and "pursue," imply an urgency, a great desire, a strong drive. You cannot expect righteousness to just come to you, but you must be willing to "pursue" it. That pursuit begins with a decision to be obedient. Paul wrote, "… you are slaves to sin, which leads to death, or to obedience, which leads to righteousness." (Rom. 6: 16 NIV) The road to righteousness follows the path of obedience.

The pursuit of righteousness also requires discipline. "No discipline seems pleasant at the time, but painful. Later on, however, it produces a harvest of righteousness and peace for those who have been trained by it." (Heb. 12:11 NIV) It also requires training from God's Word. "All Scripture is God-breathed and is useful for teaching, rebuking, correcting and training in righteousness, so that the man of God may be thoroughly equipped for every good work." (II Tim. 3:16 NIV)

Those who pursue righteousness are blessed, for they will be righteous. However, it is not their pursuit that causes them to catch it or achieve it, but rather, it is because they "hunger and thirst" after it, that God gives it to them. Paul speaks of "God's abundant provision of grace and of the gift of righteousness" in Romans chapter 5. "For in the gospel a righteousness from God is revealed, a righteousness that is by faith…." (Rom. 1:17 NIV) "This righteousness from God comes by faith in Jesus Christ to all who believe…for all have sinned and fall short of the glory of God, and are justified freely by His grace through the redemption that came by Christ Jesus. (Rom. 3:22-24 NIV) "Now when a man works, his wages are not credited to him as a gift, but as an obligation. However, to the man who does not work but trusts God who justifies the wicked, his faith is credited as righteousness." (Rom. 4:4-5 NIV)

To summarize, those who pursue righteousness will find Christ, and His righteousness will be attributed to them by their faith in Him. Therefore, they will most assuredly be blessed. Psalm 84:10-11 (NIV) says, "For the Lord God is a sun and shield; the Lord bestows favor and honor; no good things does He withhold from those whose walk is blameless. O Lord Almighty, blessed is the man who trusts in you."

Fifth, "blessed are the merciful, for they will be shown mercy." Mercy involves kindness, compassion and forgiveness. Paul wrote, "Be kind and compassionate to one another, forgiving each other, just as in Christ God forgave you." (Eph. 4:32 NIV) Man's greatest need is for mercy, for if Holy God gives us what we deserve, we are doomed. If we are merciful, we will receive mercy and therefore we are blessed.

Sixth, "blessed are the pure in heart, for they will see God." Jeremiah 17:9 says, "The heart is deceitful above all things, and desperately wicked." So how can one be pure in heart?—Only by receiving God's forgiveness. David wrote in Psalm 51, "Cleanse me with hyssop, and I will be clean; wash me and I will be whiter than snow. Create in me a **pure heart**, O God, and renew a steadfast spirit within me." A pure heart can only come as a result of God's working in that heart. If your heart is pure, you are blessed and you will see God.

Seventh, "Blessed are the peacemakers, for they will be called sons of God." A peacemaker is one who has the ability and makes the effort to reduce turmoil and strife. Peace is one of the fruits of the Spirit, so the Spirit in a Christian will prompt that man or woman to promote peace. We also know that those who are led by the Spirit are sons of God, (Rom. 8:14) so it makes sense that they will be called sons of God. Jesus himself is the "Prince of Peace" (Is. 9:6) and the good news of His death and resurrection is the gospel of peace. (Ephesians 6) The best way for you to be a peacemaker is to give out the gospel of peace. That gospel message will bring peace to the hearts of those who believe.

Finally Christ tells us, "Blessed are those who are persecuted because of righteousness, for theirs is the kingdom of heaven." This truth is another paradox, for certainly it is not immediately obvious. If we are persecuted because we do right, how can we consider that a blessing? When we are persecuted for being righteous, our persecution is a sign of our identification with Christ. Jesus said, "Remember the words I spoke to you: 'No servant is greater than his master.' If they persecuted me, they will persecute you also. If they obeyed my teaching, they will obey yours also. They will treat you this way because of my name, for they do not know the One who sent me." Paul wrote, "In fact, everyone who wants to live a godly life in Christ Jesus will be persecuted." (II Tim. 3:12) Therefore, our persecution identifies us with Christ, and since we are in Christ, the kingdom of heaven is ours.

Jesus expounds on this lesson. "Blessed are you when people insult you, persecute you and falsely say all kinds of evil against you because of me." Verbal or physical abuse that you experience because of your identification with Christ brings you a blessing. Therefore, Christ continues, "Rejoice and be glad, because great is your reward in heaven, for in the same way they persecuted the prophets who were before you." When is the last time you obeyed this instruction and rejoiced and became glad when you were insulted or persecuted for righteousness? We tend to get irritated, angry or combative, but Jesus instructs us to rejoice and be glad. Recall that "we share in His suffering in order that we may also share in His glory." (Rom. 8:17b) Remember this the next time you are persecuted.

So then, if you desire God's richest blessing upon you and your efforts, you need not directly pursue that blessing, but instead pursue the things that will guarantee you His blessing. They are the knowledge of your spiritual need, a concern for the hurts and needs of mankind, humility before God, righteousness, a merciful attitude, a pure heart, peace, and a joyful attitude in persecution. As you become consumed by this endeavor, you will become the man described in Psalm 1:1-2. "Blessed is the man who does not walk in the counsel of the wicked or stand in the way of sinners or sit in the seat of mockers. But his delight is in the law of the Lord, and on His law he meditates day and night." As you become that man, verse 3 will apply to you: "He is like a tree planted by streams of water, which yields its fruit in season and whose leaf does not wither. Whatever he does prospers."

There is a principle that is evident in the blessing of God. I call this the principle of multiplied blessing. I have seen it in the lives of athletes and it is also apparent in the lives of Old Testament saints. Jesus referred to it when he said, "I tell you the truth, no one who has left home or brothers or sisters or mother or father or children or fields for Me and the gospel will fail to receive a hundred times as much in this age…and in the age to come, eternal life." (Mark 10:29-30 NIV)

It is no surprise that a loving father who allows his child to sacrifice or suffer for a short time, either for his own good or the good of someone else, will, after that time, give a proportionally greater blessing to that child if he has borne the hardship with a Christ-like attitude.

We see this in the example of Job, who suffered greatly at the hands of Satan, with God's permission. Yet, "in all this Job sinned not, nor charged God foolishly." (Job 1:22 NIV) Therefore, after Job had proved himself faithful, "the Lord gave Job twice as much as he had before." The seven thousand sheep he had lost were replaced by fourteen thousand sheep. His three thousand lost camels were replaced by six thousand new camels, and so on with all his cattle. And he gained another family of seven sons and three daughters, just as before. However, his children, as opposed to his cattle, were eternal beings, so Job actually had twice the children as well. Half were already in the safety of heaven.

Think of Joshua, who was faithful to God but was forced back into the wilderness for forty years because of the sins of the ten spies. Forty years later he not only entered the Promised Land, but God blessed him to lead the entire nation of Israel into the land of Canaan. The same principle is seen in God's blessings in the lives of Caleb, Joseph, Daniel, and many others. Faithfulness in times of limited blessing is rewarded with multiplied blessings down the road. In the words of the Master, "You have been faithful over a little. I will set you over much."

So when it appears that God is withholding His blessing, stay faithful and look ahead, expecting the greater blessing which surely lies ahead. The blessing of God on your life is indeed a very wonderful thing. However, you often need mature spiritual eyes to see God's blessing, for His blessing is not only in victories. Sometimes a defeat may be a blessing from God. Genesis 39:23 says, "...the Lord was with Joseph and gave him success in whatever he did." How would you like to have that said of you? When I used to read that, I always thought, that's what I want for my life, but then one day I realized that this statement was made about Joseph while he was in prison. Was that really what I wanted? The same was spoken about David, for we read in I Samuel 18:14 "In everything he did he had great success, because the Lord was with him." That sure sounds great, doesn't it? However, just three verses earlier you can read that Saul hurled a spear at David, trying to pin him to the wall. This was not a time when David had everything he wished for.

So you can see that success does not mean that all your life will be smooth sailing and all things will go according to your desires. God's blessing does not mean that you will get everything that you want in this life. But most of the things you wish for pale in comparison to what you have in Christ, "an inheritance that can never perish, spoil or fade—kept in heaven for you, who through faith are shielded by God's power until the coming of the salvation that is ready to be revealed in the last time. In this you greatly rejoice, though now for a little while you may have had to suffer grief in all kinds of trials. These have come so that your faith—of greater worth than gold, which perishes even though refined by fire—may be proved genuine and may result in praise, glory and honor when Jesus Christ is revealed." (I Pet. 1:4-7 NIV)

You will receive "the crown of righteousness, which the Lord, the righteous judge, will award ... on that day ...to all who have longed for His appearing." (II Tim. 4:8 NIV) Though you may not be wealthy in this life, you are co-heirs with Christ of all that belongs to God the Father. Though you may not have perfect health, you will live forever. Though your vision may not be perfect, you can see the truth. The surrendered Christian athlete has the blessing of God upon him. What a great way to live your life. Are you truly surrendered to Him? If not, what are you waiting for?

Chapter 18
The Joy of Service

It seems they are at every significant sporting event. Surely you have seen them. They appear for an instant and then they are gone. Often you will not even remember that you have seen them. Maybe you saw them first at a basketball game. Perhaps a player forced up a shot in traffic, and though the shot went in, the player crashed to the floor. As he got up and headed with the other players down the court, there they came—probably two of them, with towels in their hands, wiping up the floor with energy and enthusiasm that surpassed that of the basketball players themselves. With their job quickly and efficiently completed, they sprinted back to the sideline. You may not even have taken note of them, but if you did, you undoubtedly were struck by the zeal they brought to their menial task. Were these the same youngsters who complained when dad asked them to pick up the clothes that were on the floor in their room? Were these the same children that wouldn't think of washing the kitchen floor for mom? Why then this sudden apparent love of wiping up sweat?

Or perhaps you noticed them first when watching a tennis match on television. The ball hit the net and dropped to the court. Suddenly, from offstage came a young track star, or at least someone sprinting with all the effort of a track star. It may have been a boy or girl, but surely the person was young. The phantom grabbed the ball off the court and in an instant was gone, and the match went on.

Almost every sport has them, but they generally go unnoticed and they are rarely appreciated. Nevertheless, young kids will line up for those jobs. They may be called ball boys, bat girls, water boys, or managers. Often they are younger brothers or sisters of an athlete on the team. Yet, all they do is serve the athletes, almost always without compensation. So then, from where does the joy, excitement, energy and enthusiasm come?

Obviously it is not the work they are doing that creates the excitement. Rather, it is the athletes whom they are having the privilege of serving. That's right. I said the "privilege of serving." These young people generally idolize the team members they are serving. They want to grow up to be just like their hero on that team. In a sense, they worship those athletes, and therefore they are thrilled to just be associated in any way with their heroes, even if it means serving them in the most unglamorous ways.

Now I ask you, should we not do the same for God? Will the surrendered Christian athlete not serve the Lord with joy? The more you come to understand what the Lord did for you and the more you grow to love Him, the more you will want to serve Him. Although He certainly does not need you to serve Him, your service to Him is a demonstration of your love for Him, and He delights in it even as a father delights in his children's love. Picture a young son cheerfully meeting his father at the car as he arrives home from work. The son offers to carry the father's briefcase to the house for him. This brings the father delight, not because he needs help with his briefcase, but because the son is showing his love for him. The same is true of God the Father. "The Lord your God is with you, He is mighty to save. He will take great delight in you, He will quiet you with His love, He will rejoice over you with singing. (Zeph. 3:17 NIV) Surely the opportunity to delight the Savior that you love will bring joy to your heart. When you are able to do something that brings happiness to someone you love, that is a source of joy for you. When that Someone is your Creator, your Redeemer, and your Sanctifier, it should be the source of your greatest joy. If your love for the Lord is real, it should be easy for you to obey the command of Psalm 100, "Serve the Lord with gladness...."

Assume that Jesus came back to this earth as a man to live for a few days. If you know and love the Lord, I'm sure you would be most happy to serve Him and meet His needs in whatever way possible. If He was hungry, you'd gladly prepare something for Him to eat. If He was sick, you would try to help Him in whatever way you could. If He needed transportation, you would cheerfully give Him a ride. However, Jesus is not here in the flesh, and so you cannot serve Him physically. However, His Word tells us that He will one day say, "I tell you the truth, whatever you did for one of the least of these brothers of mine, you did for Me." (Matt. 26:40 NIV) When you show your love for Christ by loving and serving others, you are serving Him. Though you are not serving Him directly, you are serving Him indirectly, and the surrendered Christian athlete will spend his life doing this.

Thankfully, you can also serve the Lord directly. How can you do that? What do you have to give Him that He does not already own? What service could you perform for Him that would in any way benefit Him?

There are actually a few things the Lord desires that He does not necessarily have, and the only way He can get them is if you give them to Him. He desires your fellowship, He desires your praise, and He desires your love. He does not necessarily have these things because in creation God gave man a free will; that is, the ability to make his own choices. The result was that God risked receiving what He desired—for which He created man—to share fellowship and love with Him. Though God loves everyone, not everyone loves God. He certainly loves you, but whether or not you return that love is up to you. The choice is yours. In this regard, God is "pro-choice," because he chose to give you a choice, a free will. You can accept God's love, His plan and His way, or you can turn your back on all of them.

Joshua implored the people he was leading to make this choice. "…choose for yourselves this day whom you will serve… But as for me and my household, we will serve the Lord." (Josh. 24:15 NIV)

By properly serving the Lord you are giving God what He desires. But what specifically does He desire from you?

"Behold, Thou desirest truth in the inward being," says Psalm 51:6 (RSV). When you live a life of integrity, you are serving the Lord. "I desire mercy, not sacrifice." (Matt. 9:13, Matt. 12:7) When you live a life of showing mercy, you are serving the Lord. "Everyone should be quick to listen, slow to speak and slow to become angry, for man's anger does not bring about the righteous life that God desires." (James 1:20 NIV) When you live a life of pursuing righteousness, you are serving the Lord.

"I don't want your sacrifices—I want your love; I don't want your offerings—I want you to know me." (Hosea 6:6 TLB) When you live a life pursuing an increased knowledge of God and a growing love for God, you are serving Him. Paul prayed this for the Christians in Colosse, "in order that (they might) live a life worthy of the Lord and may please Him in every way: bearing fruit in every good work, growing in the knowledge of God." (Col. 1:10 NIV)

In fact, whatever we do according to God's will we can do as service to the Lord. Paul exhorts Christians, "Whatever you do, work at it with all your heart, as working for the Lord, not for men, since you know that you will receive an inheritance from the Lord as a reward. It is the Lord Christ you are serving." (Col. 3:23-24 NIV)

Yes, indeed, daily we have many opportunities to serve the Lord. What a privilege! What a source of joy! Yes, because of who God is, there is joy in serving Him. If this concept were fully understood, it alone would be enough to fill all our service with joy. However, there are also several other considerations that can contribute to an attitude of joyful service to the Christian.

Consider that when you serve you are following the example of your hero, Jesus Christ. As we examined earlier, Paul wrote, "Have this mind among yourselves, which is yours in Christ Jesus, who, though He was in the form of God, did not count equality with

God a thing to be grasped, but emptied Himself, taking the form of a servant…." (Phil. 2:5-7 RSV) Jesus Himself said, "…the Son of Man did not come to be served, but to serve, and to give his life a ransom for many." (Matt. 21:28 NIV) He demonstrated this throughout his life and ministry but especially made this point for His disciples when He washed their feet. Then He said, "Now that I, your Lord and teacher, have washed your feet, you also should wash one another's feet. I have set you an example that you should do as I have done. I tell you the truth, no servant is greater than his master, nor is a messenger greater than the one who sent him." (John 13:14-16 NIV) Certainly it is a joy for a Christian when he can be just like Jesus.

Consider also that when you serve, you are fulfilling one of the main purposes for which God placed you on earth. "For we are God's workmanship, created in Christ Jesus to do good works, which God prepared in advance for us to do." (Eph. 2:10 NIV) And again Paul said that God called some men as apostles, some as prophets, some as evangelists, and some as pastors and teachers, "to prepare God's people for works of service…." There is a joy in fulfilling your purpose, and you should feel that joy when you serve.

Consider as well that when you serve you are taking advantage of your opportunities to use the gifts God has given you, and when you do that, you honor Him. If you give a friend a gift, you feel pleased and honored if that friend delights in that gift and uses it often. Peter exhorts us, "Each one should use whatever gift he has received to serve others, faithfully administering God's grace in its various forms. If anyone speaks, he should do it as one speaking the very words of God. If anyone serves, he should do it with the strength God provides, so that in all things God may be praised through Jesus Christ. To Him be the glory and the power forever and ever. Amen." (I Pet. 4: 10-11 NIV)

Consider next that when you serve as God has planned, you are guaranteed success because all of God's plans will be accomplished. "The Lord Almighty has sworn, 'Surely, as I have planned, so it will be, and as I have purposed, so it will stand." (Is. 14:24 NIV) And yet again, "What I have said, that will I bring about; what I have planned, that will I do." (Is. 46: 11b NIV) So when you serve the Lord, you have the joy of knowing that God's plans are being accomplished through you.

Consider, finally, that when you are a faithful servant, you are earning additional opportunities for greater responsibilities. We have seen that the master told the faithful servants, "You have been faithful with a few things; I will put you in charge of many things." (Matt. 25:21, 23 NIV) Jesus Himself told His disciples, "The greatest among you should be like the youngest, and the one who rules like the one who serves. For who is greater, the one who is at the table or the one who serves? Is it not the one who is at the table? But I am among you as one who serves.... And I confer on you a kingdom, just as my Father conferred one on me, so that you may eat and drink at my table in my kingdom and sit on thrones, judging the twelve tribes of Israel." (Luke 22: 26-30 NIV) "Here is a trustworthy saying: If we died with Him, we will also live with Him; if we endure, we will also reign with Him." (II Tim. 2:11-12a NIV) Christ's servants will be honored. The Lord said, "Whoever serves me must follow me; and where I am, my servant also will be. My Father will honor the one who serves me." (John 12: 26 NIV) Should it not bring you joy to think that you will reign with Christ and the Father will honor you?

The stadium is filled to capacity. Another ten million people are watching by television. You are standing with your two toughest competitors in the middle of the arena. All eyes are upon you. As each of the other two names is called, the athlete steps up onto the podium, receives the medal, and acknowledges the applause of the spectators. Then you hear your name, loud and clear over the public address system. You are the champion. You step to the top of the podium. The crowd roars its approval. Your national anthem begins to play. As a reverent hush falls over the audience, you fight back the tears. At that moment, all your training seems worth it. All the struggles and hardships that you have endured are forgotten in the joy of the moment. You think: Perhaps this is my greatest moment. As an athlete, you may already have experienced such a moment or perhaps one day still in the future such a moment is reserved for you, but probably not. The reality is that the number of athletes striving to reach such a pinnacle and the number that actually do are vastly different, but don't let that discourage you. Work hard to reach the highest possible level in athletics and in whatever else God calls you to do. You will be able to accomplish everything that He has planned for you, and He has some great things in mind for you.

Ten billion souls and countless angels have their complete attention focused upon the proceedings. Your name is called, loud and clear, like a roar of thunder but without a public address system. You are suddenly standing in front of the crowd, before the throne of God. You fall on your face and a reverent hush falls over the audience. God opens the book of life and finds your name there. He recounts the ways that you have served Him during your lifetime. "I was hungry and you gave me something to eat, I was thirsty and you gave me something to drink, I was a stranger and you invited me in, I needed clothes and you clothed me, I was sick and you looked after me, I was in prison and you came to visit me." (Matt. 25: 35-36 NIV) "Well done, good and faithful servant! You have been faithful over a few things, I will make you ruler over many things. Enter into the joy of your Lord." (Matt: 25: 21) At that moment all the struggles and hardships that you have endured are forgotten in the all-surpassing joy of the moment. You know, "This is my greatest moment." You have achieved ultimate success, for you have heard the Lord say to you, "Well done, good and faithful servant." No words can surpass those words. No success, athletic or other, can surpass that success. You have reached the pinnacle of your potential.

If you are a surrendered Christian athlete you will experience such a moment, as will all those who put their faith in Christ. It will make any moment of athletic honor with which God may bless your life seem insignificant. So then, as you train, work and serve toward that day, may the joy of the Lord be your strength. There is indeed victory in surrender, when you surrender to Him.